SWINDON
in the NEWS

Christ Church, 'the Old Lady on the Hill', celebrated its centenary in 1951.

SWINDON
in the NEWS

JOHN & LINDA HUDSON

First published in the United Kingdom in 2002 by
Sutton Publishing Limited exclusively for
WHSmith, Greenbridge Road, Swindon SN3 3LD

British Library Cataloguing in Publication Data
A catalogue record for this book is available from the British Library.

ISBN 0-7509-3127-2

Illustrations

Front endpaper: Roller skating party at the old Corn Exchange, 1911.
Back endpaper: Tranquil times at Coate Water.
Half title page: Workers stream from the GWR Works.
Title page: The Town Hall with the Baptist Tabernacle on the right, some fifty years ago.

Typeset in 11/14pt Photina and produced by
Sutton Publishing Limited, Phoenix Mill,
Thrupp, Stroud, Gloucestershire GL5 2BU.
Printed and bound in England by
J.H. Haynes & Co. Ltd, Sparkford.

The Corn Exchange – a building in peril.

Contents

The Town Hall, the war memorial – and trees. Trees are very important in the Swindon area these days.

Introduction

In 2001, when the National Trust announced that it was to devolve from London to Swindon, we discovered that all the snobbery and prejudice we thought had died out years ago was still there, bubbling away not very far at all beneath the surface. One National Trust staff member quoted in the national press said: 'I abhor Swindon. I will just get another job.' Another called it 'just the worst place on earth'. It is hard to think of many other communities that would evoke such virulent comments. Scunthorpe or Wigan, perhaps, doubtless equally unjustly, though at least they have the disadvantage of vaguely comical names. What's so funny about Swindon?

It has a lot to do with metropolitan superciliousness. When people were less mobile, the most available west-of-London provincials to look down upon, and invoke friendly bombs

All is not changed. A century has made little impact on the outward appearance of the Goddard Arms in Old Town.

The towering David Murray John Building – and trees.

Pedestrianisation works. This was once a traffic-clogged corner of Regent Street.

to rain down upon, were the people of Slough; later, Reading became the butt of humour; Swindon came next; and as burgeoning Chippenham gets to be talked of more and more as a 'mini-Swindon', this might be the time and place to say look out, chaps, it's your turn next . . .

What Swindon has is what most towns would envy: stability (as much as anyone can expect it in this uncertain world), low unemployment, world-beating industries and road and rail links second to none. The old joke about this being an easy place to get out of grows increasingly tiresome, but it is based on firm facts. Good communications are what every community craves, and in Swindon we have them, whether it is for commerce or leisure.

Growth in manufacturing has been marked in recent years, and Honda has had a lot to do with that; but it is a long time since Swindon was a single-industry town, and that has never been less the case than now. Fifty years ago, when the writing was on the wall for the Railway Works, there were substantial providers of work in Vickers Armstrong, Garrard, Plessey, R.A. Lister, Wills, Compton's and other clothing manufacturers. Now scores of electronics and IT-based companies operate here, as well as leading names in food processing, packaging, pharmaceuticals and the financial and service industries.

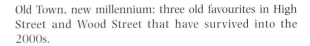

Old Town, new millennium: three old favourites in High
Street and Wood Street that have survived into the
2000s.

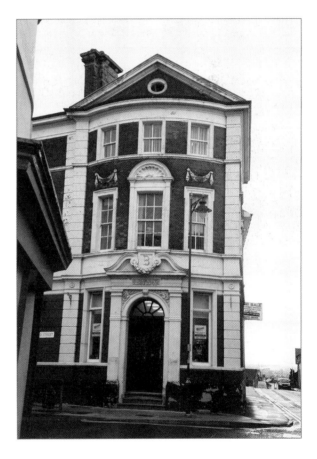

The cogs of commerce keep turning in the Great Western Outlet Village.

The time is not far distant when Swindon will boast a population of 200,000-plus. What is more important than whether or not it can call itself a city is how it can provide for this very large number of people, many of them making their home here from elsewhere. They join a local population that is proud of its achievement in staving off an employment crisis when the Railway Works closed. They also join a community surrounded by beautiful countryside, and eager to make it even more so through its woodland renewal plans. There is a lively theatre, more cinema seats per person than in any other town in the country, so they say, and shopping centres that pull in the crowds from miles around. Not only does the council take old-fashioned good care of Old Town Gardens and our other great parks, but we the people still take good care of them, too. We love the Museum and Art Gallery and are impressed by the scale and grandeur of Steam, while wondering quite how it will balance its books in the years ahead.

Let us not pretend, though, that this is the only cause for concern. If we saw buildings such as the Corn Exchange, the Old Town Hall and the Mechanics' Institute rotting away in some eastern European country as they are now doing here, we would be horrified and swear that it could not happen in Swindon. But it can happen in Swindon and it does, in a way that baffles and distresses not only the town's older residents. Buildings that have been allowed to deteriorate to that extent have very little time left to them before they are either rescued or die.

In the end, though, it is the people who make a town. They say human nature never really changes, but just how would we relate to those who went before us if we could step into some of the old photographs in this book? What is certain is that it would be a steep learning curve for both us and them.

This book aims to touch upon some of the topics Swindon people were talking about in every year of the last century, whether momentous or trivial. The rationale behind the inclusion of some of them is that there really is nothing new under the sun. We hope you join us in believing that though this may be yesterday's news, it still has a great deal to tell us.

Before the First World War

T he century could hardly have begun on a much more auspicious note for Swindon, with the merging into a single entity of the traditional Old Town and the New Town that developed from the coming of the railways in the 1830s. The charter was signed by Queen Victoria on 22 January 1900 and municipal borough status was granted on 9 November creating, at 45,000, the most heavily populated local authority in Wiltshire. There was no doubt where the balance of power lay. Before the merger, the two communities were run by boards, and in 1890 the New Town board had spent £9,000 on the splendid red-brick pile that dominates Regent Circus. The borough needed to look no further for its Town Hall, and the new order made further inroads when the first mayor, selected unanimously, was George Churchward, a mightily effective and influential works

The Town Hall: £9,000 well spent.

manager of the Great Western Railway Works. He had headed the field in the poll for the Queen's ward; in fact he had polled more votes than any other candidate anywhere in the election. Unusually for a mayor, Churchward was a bachelor, and the *North Wilts Herald* reported somewhat breathlessly that 'already there is much conjecture amongst the burgesses as to who will be the Mayoress'. In fact, such considerations were of scant concern for this no-nonsense man. At the first council meeting under his new leadership it was decided that there would be no fireworks or church parades to herald the new authority. The emphasis was on modernisation, and the first objective was to usher Swindon into the new world of electric tramcars and street lighting; it was not long before residents began to see results.

THE HEROES RETURN

As the *North Wilts Herald* reported, the town was 'in gay garb' for the return of the Royal Wiltshire Yeomanry from the Boer War on 9 July 1901. There were thousands on the streets in bright sunshine, packed so tight that it was hard for the procession to carve a path through them all the way from the GWR station to the Town Hall, and buildings were decked with flowers, bunting and welcome home messages. The Railway Hotel in Newport Street caught the eye in particular, and at night the building was lit with a large gas jet in the form of a crown and several hundred fairy lights. The station 'had been very prettily dressed by the station-master', and from there the returning men rode to the Town Hall on horses supplied 'through the kindness of several local gentlemen'. Mounted police and the Yeomanry Band playing *See the Conquering Hero Come* led the march, followed by the men and then the band of the Wilts Volunteer Battalion, a drum and fife band and finally local volunteers with the active servicemen plus a few members of the St John Ambulance Brigade. In the Town Hall the Mayor, Deputy Mayor, Corporation and a 'bevy of ladies' welcomed them enthusiastically, while the orchestra of the Queen's Theatre played in the gallery. After speeches and refreshments there was a rendition of *God Save the King* – although the words still did not come easily to many after more than sixty years of *God Save the Queen*! The men then filed out again into Regent Circus, where the crowd was still waiting patiently for them, and a huge cheer went up as they reappeared. Horses were remounted, and all progressed to the Market Square, where Colonel H. Bevir of the Wiltshire Regiment's Volunteer Battalion expressed satisfaction at their safe return. 'Men were then dismissed, and speedily made prisoners by their friends,' the *Herald* concluded, in a phrase that rather neatly implied 'and about time, too'. What it did not explain was the fact that although the Yeomanry were home, the Boer War was by no means over. That did not come about until May the following year, and there were more comings and goings of men at railway stations before the 'gay garb' could be worn with conviction.

The coronation of Edward VII on 9 August 1902 came just weeks after the end of the Boer War, which the history books at least record as a British victory; it had not always seemed like one at the time, but it seemed an extra reason to celebrate, which Swindon did in a somewhat dutiful, well-organised kind of way. There were decorations and illuminations, and it was a pity that the Grand Sports Meeting at the County Ground on the Friday was marred by rain until the evening. There were races and competitions on both

Two views of Commercial Road at around the time of the coronation of Edward VII. There is not too much celebratory joy captured in these pictures – and not too much commercial activity, either.

the cricket and football grounds, but many people got more joy from the GWR children's fête the following day. Other events included a dinner for the old people and a rather half-hearted procession which did not impress the onlookers much; but where Swindon always seemed to score in those days was in decorating and lighting the streets – not least, perhaps, because there were cash prizes for the best displays in various categories. 'Dusk set in and thousands of fairy lights shone forth from housetop to cellar, from street to street,' reported the *North Wilts Herald* in a touching little evocation of a special summer evening a hundred years ago.

In the early years of the century fund-raising bazaars could go on for days if a church, sports club or society was feeling the need for a cash injection. The Bath Road Methodist Church in particular used to throw itself into them wholeheartedly, and its members remembered for years the great Far East extravaganza of November 1903. The Corn Exchange was transformed into a Japanese street scene, with 'native houses made of bamboo, with lattice work, matting and palm leaf roofs and sides'. Stalls with colourful signs carried such evocative names as the Rising Sun of Tokio, the Flower of Yesso, the Sweet Moon of Corea and the Mimosa Tea House, a haven of rest built on white pedestals and illuminated by Chinese lanterns, where 'one could feel almost inclined to recline and sip tea among the pretty Geishas forever'. A bamboo pagoda stood some twenty feet high, soaring up towards a roof festooned with lanterns and parasols. Meanwhile, a fishing game was the big attraction in an indoor pond on which floated a bamboo raft with a junk sail some twelve feet high. A description of the general scene is still magical, a century later:

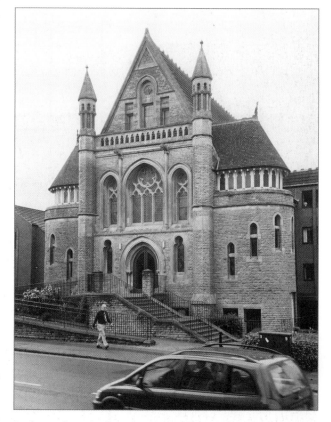

> The whole of the walls of the hall are hung with coloured muslin, nearly a thousand yards . . . Then there are over 200 Chinese lanterns . . . which are illuminated as soon as the shades of night begin to fall. Many lanterns are crimson . . . Japan rice curtains, wonderful pieces of work . . . are suspended at different points . . . The sterner sex had some difficulty in appearing at ease in their extraordinary oriental costumes with such unusual appendages hanging from their heads; but the bevy of fair Chinese and Japanese ladies, moving noiselessly about attired in the daintiest of (predominantly red and yellow) costumes, delighted all eyes.

A line at the end of the report states in almost throwaway fashion that the dresses had been made by Messrs Liberty & Co. of London, 'and reflected the highest credit on that firm'; only the best, clearly, for the Bath Road Methodist ladies of 1903.

Bath Road Methodist Church is still a centre of local life in Old Town, now part of a wider ecumenical parish.

One of a series of disasters in the early years of the century: the Blunsdon Abbey fire of 22 April 1904.

Blunsdon also had its more peaceful and relaxing aspects at around that time.

THE TRAMS ROLL IN

After much disruption as poles to carry the overhead power cables (and electric street lamps) were put up, Swindon's tram service opened on 22 September 1904. There had been a tramway committee from day one of the unified borough council late in 1900, and it had worked quickly. The London company J.G. White had laid the tracks to a 3ft 6in gauge, and the first batch of nine cars came from the Preston makers Dick, Kerr, who came up with a tried and tested 48-passenger model on Brill 21E trucks. Electricity aside, there was a buzz in the air generally around town that bright autumn day, especially at the junction of Bridge Street and Fleet Street, henceforth to be known as the tramway's Centre. The sparkling new maroon and cream cars lined up nose-to-tail for the ceremony, crammed with guests who had lunched at the railway station refreshment rooms, and the mayor, Alderman James Hinton, took a symbolic turn at the wheel of No. 1. All did not quite run smoothly. The mishap did not equal that of 1830, when Stephenson's *Rocket* knocked down and killed the President of the Board of Trade at the opening of the Liverpool & Manchester Railway, but there was still consternation when the first service car somehow rounded the corner at the Centre too sharply and its trolley lost contact with the overhead wire. The passengers had to dismount and take another tram, while the reception committee waiting at the Town Hall could only stand and wonder what disaster had befallen them.

There was a genuine disaster on the evening of 1 June 1906, shortly after the corporation had bought three bigger 54-passenger Brush vehicles for use on two new routes, from the station to the Corn Exchange in Old Town and from Rodbourne and Gorse Hill. One of these, No. 11, suffered brake failure on Victoria Hill while packed with people going home from the Bath & West Show at Broome Manor; five people were killed and thirty injured when it was derailed and crashed at points near the Town Hall. In fact a fault had been reported an hour earlier, but a fitter sent to the Corn Exchange to look at

Huge crowds turned out for the running of the first tram, on 22 September 1904.

The great tram disaster of 1 June 1906.

it had been dismissed by the motorman. There was a crisis in confidence in the service for a while after that, especially among older folk, and in the longer term compensation payments had their impact on the town's rates for years to come. On a slightly lighter note, word on the street had it that one of the survivors grumbled that he had only just paid his fare before the crash happened; if the tram had crashed two minutes earlier he would have been 'tuppence in pocket'. But the trams certainly earned their keep: figures for the first three weeks of 1908 showed they carried 38,000-plus passengers per week, with weekly takings of around £130.

Victoria Road (then and still better known as Victoria Hill), not far from the scene of the accident.

It is easy to overlook the dangers of everyday life a hundred years ago. Some people complain about today's 'nanny state', though none but the hardiest of modern folk would tolerate the hazards of merely walking out on to the Edwardian street and going to work: there were road excavations, workmen's braziers, unlit corners, an increasingly lethal mix of motorised and horse-drawn vehicles, unreliable gas supplies, unsound, worn-out buildings and unguarded machinery. And that was just when you were going about your normal business. When things went wrong in your life, it could all get a great deal worse. One day in October 1905 a porter at Shrub Hill railway station in Worcester found a cold, shivering thirteen-year-old Swindon boy called Arthur Siddons clinging to the couplings of a southbound train. It would be good to think he was given food and a hot bath before he was charged with riding without a ticket, but the *North Wilts Herald*'s report makes no mention of that. His story, as it unravelled, began to read like something out of a Dickens novel. After his postal inspector father had been sent to prison for tampering with parcels, the boy was put in the workhouse while enquiries were made. Arthur wanted to stay in Swindon with his stepmother in Handel Street. She found work at Compton's clothing factory while he worked as a newsboy, but something went wrong and he made off to see his grandfather in Birmingham. Before long he was on his travels again, once more unannounced. When he was found at Worcester, he had walked from Birmingham to Droitwich and then jumped on to the couplings of a train bound for Cheltenham, with an eventual return to Swindon presumably in mind.

SUN AT LAST AT THE SHOW

The Bath & West Show came to Swindon in 1906 and was held at Broome Farm, near Coate Water, in late May and early June. It was a new venue and as the weather was poor there was no great enthusiasm until Whit Monday, when the day was at last bright and the crowds turned out in force. 'Swindon May Congratulate Itself', the *North Wilts Herald* concluded, presumably referring to the attendance figures rather than its ability to make the sun shine. At the annual meeting the Prince of Wales was elected president, and the huge beef cattle seemed to catch the townsfolk's imagination more than most. That said, it was the tram disaster of 1 June that year that coloured people's views of the success or failure of the show more than anything else. One wonders which is the better way to learn about events in one's own community: through a single news report, followed by endless word-of-mouth stories and rumours, or via the blanket coverage that local press, television and radio would give such a disaster today. It is easy to imagine that the haphazard process of a hundred years ago would add up to a more confusing and frightening picture in which a little knowledge could be a very disturbing thing. As it turned out, the 1906 accident was the only fatal one in the twenty-five years the trams were running.

On a lighter note that year T. Smallbone of the Ship Hotel in Westcott Place begged to intimate that he had just purchased a magnificent full-sized BILLIARD TABLE, with a Patent Arrangement for Returning Balls and All Latest Accessories: 'A comfortable BILLIARD SALOON has been fitted up, and the kind patronage of his friends, customers and the public generally is cordially solicited.'

Dignitaries at the Bath & West Show at Broome Farm, photographed the day before the tram crash in 1906.

An astonishing lightning flash seen over the night sky at 1.15am on a June morning in 1906. What was Mr Hooper the photographer doing out and about at that time?

At least these young men took their sport seriously in 1907.

FOOTBALL FOOLERY

Light-hearted football matches played for charity were quite a feature of life in the first half of the twentieth century. Arsenal had quite a reputation for staging them, with such encounters as Boxers v Jockeys, and so on – and they clung on until not very long ago with Showbiz XIs. One reason they have all but died out is that the Showbiz players became so obscure that their names meant nothing to most onlookers. The other is that it's a fool's game watching men who cannot play football trying to do so, and the fact that they once played bass guitar for Dave Dee, Dozy, Beaky, Mick and Tich makes the spectacle none the more edifying. There were no such qualms in the Swindon of old, however, when the Annual Comic Football Match was quite a little money-spinner. In April 1907 £15 10s was raised at the gate and as much in pre-match ticket sales. The sale of flowers contributed 13s 6d, while another 6s 10d was made by Bruce the dog of the Volunteer Band. The *North Wilts Herald* seemed to enjoy the occasion, but not the sport. 'That which occupied the attentions of the onlookers for the most part was supposed to be a football match between the artistes and representatives of the Fire Brigade, but a considerable stretch of the imagination was required in order to realise that such was the case,' it noted:

It was a contest in which those absolutely indifferent towards and unacquainted with the conventional game could take a tolerable interest. Whilst the ball used was that usually employed in the association game, the code adopted was nondescript; and although the ground had been marked out in accordance with the recognised rules, there was a strange discrepancy between the numerical strength of the sides. The Fire Brigade had 11 men, but the artistes served up about 16 – sometimes more, sometimes less. There was a referee, who held a whistle, and three linesmen were on duty. The function of the odd one was probably that of a relief man. The result of the battle lacked the quality of being definite. Whether the score was three to one or 11 to six in favour of either side was hardly clear. It was not that the decisions of the whistle holder were not 'understood of the people', but there was a general incongruity of method, which at times degenerated into no method at all, that was puzzling to everybody. At three o'clock the Mayor commenced operations with a big kick. Thenceforward things proceeded merrily. Some members of the Fire Brigade team took things sufficiently seriously to remove their thick jackets, and Deputy Captain Grubb set a good example by a display of untiring energy. They were called upon to fill the dual capacity of playing football and acting as entertainers. The majority of them fell short of their obligations and merely heeded the second function. The game was not characterised by any long-sustained continuity, and the artistes particularly were not always disposed to kick the same way. One of their numbers was very clever as a tumbler, and others indulged in curious antics. The referee was most devoted to his duties until his attention was diverted by the arrival of a bulky parcel. He suddenly engaged with great assiduity in the removal of the wrapper, upon which the contents were revealed to be a large hose. During a protracted interval the Fire Brigade gave a few wet and dry drills with the steam engine. They were handicapped by an inadequate supply of water, but the men performed with every credit. Time for the second portion of the game eventually came, and the crowd were thoroughly delighted with the lighter vein which characterised the proceedings. One of the funniest incidents happened when the artistes were given a penalty. The artiste given the honour of taking the kick was about to operate when he received the full force of the hose.

DIY CHIMNEY SWEEPING

You ran the risk of falling foul of the law if your chimney caught fire in Edwardian times. Frederick Cox of Dean Street was summoned in 1908 for wilfully setting a chimney on fire, and pleaded guilty. PC Chappell told the court that at six o'clock in the morning on Sunday 9 February he saw flames and smoke coming from Cox's chimney, and he and PC Pike went inside. They saw no fire in the grate, but a quantity of burned paper there. PC Pike asked the defendant if he had set it on fire and he replied: 'Yes. It's no use having a sweep here.' The chairman said it was a very serious matter, and the defendant would have to pay 5*s* and 7*s* costs. On the same day, for allowing chimneys to be on fire, Joseph Henry Giles of Cricklade Road had to pay 3*s* 6*d* towards the costs; Henry Eggleton of Whiteman Street, 3*s* 6*d*; Edward Styles of Cricklade Road, 5*s*; and Arthur Curtis of Cromby Street, 3*s* 6*d*. This was not a case of one policeman having a bee in his bonnet about chimney fires. Apart from PCs Chappell and Pike in that two-man job of arresting Frederick Cox, PCs Port, McGrath and Johnson were also on the witness stand.

EXCHANGE OF RÔLES

The grand-looking Corn Exchange in Old Town was opened in 1866, a dozen years after the adjacent Town Hall. That building lost its primary function when Old and New Towns combined in 1900 and the bulk of the power moved down the hill. At least it served

The Corn Exchange when it still had a semblance of dignity. By this time the Old and New Town councils had combined, leaving the Old Town Hall in search of a rôle.

nearly fifty years in its designated rôle, though, while the Corn Exchange's function as a corn market scarcely survived beyond the splendid public dinner on its opening day. Instead it became a meeting place: for the Vale of the White Horse Hunt's balls and social events, for carnivals, political meetings and films (from 1919 to 1949). It even, for a decade after 1909, served as a roller-skating rink. The parents of the children in our picture of a fancy dress carnival at the rink in 1911 seem to have gone to no small expense to make a spectacle of the event!

Another of Swindon's famous buildings was the Empire Theatre, and the closing night of the season in 1909 brought a packed house, with standing room only. Every artiste came in for an ovation, and

A detail of the Old Town Hall today – a high-profile building with an extremely short life expectancy if matters continue as they are.

the crowd went wild when Miss Maud Mortimer sang three songs in her very best style. Mr Manners, the theatre manager, took the opportunity to present Swindon's favourite with a handsome bouquet of flowers, and as an encore she performed *For Old Time's Sake*. Emmerson and Baldwin came in for a tremendous cheer on their final appearance: 'The applause was deafening, and they honestly deserved every encore they got. Their turn must certainly rank among the cleverest jugglers ever seen here.' Mr Manners thanked the audience for their excellent support during the season, and announced that, although the town had gone through great depression, business at the Empire had never been better. While he was handing out the bouquets, he presented himself with one for 'the better class of plays' he had been able to secure.

The Planks, beyond the Corn Exchange, then a quiet retreat just a few yards from the heart of Old Town.

HAROLD'S FAMOUS CUP FIGHTERS

No Swindon Town supporter needs to be reminded of the purple patch enjoyed by the team in the years around 1910: they were FA Cup semi-finalists in that year and again in 1912, and winners of the Southern League for the first time in the season in between, 1910/11. The inspiration of the team was Harold Fleming, a cultured inside-forward who played for England twelve times and was capped, as was the way in those days, for nine of those games. Known as 'Mr Swindon' – or just as often 'Sir Swindon' – he played for the Robins between 1907 and 1924, and is recalled today by a statue at the County Ground and by the street name Fleming Way, running away from the ground towards town. Cartoonists loved to portray him with his shirt sleeves always down and unbuttoned, flapping around his hands. The adoring Swindon crowd ignored those who said he could not head the ball or shoot, and opposing goalkeepers who believed the rumours often lived to rue the day. A teetotaller and St Mark's Church mainstay who refused to play on Good Friday and Christmas Day, Fleming also had critics who accused him of being over-elaborate and greedy. Then again, it is hard to find fault with a man who in the last FA Cup game before the First World War, against Manchester United, won the day in the last minute by picking up the ball on the half-way line, beating three defenders, centring, running on to his own centre and nipping through three more defenders to shoot home. All the

Sports cartoonists loved their footballers to have eccentricities. With Billy Meredith it was the toothpick he always chewed, while Alex James had his baggy shorts; no prizes for guessing what caught their eye about Harold Fleming, the great Swindon Town and England star of the 1910s and 1920s.

newspapers of the time said as much, so it *must* be true. What cannot be disputed is that in 1910, Town lost the FA Cup semi-final 2–0 to Newcastle at Tottenham, after beating Crystal Palace, Burnley, Spurs and Manchester City on the way. In 1912 they lost the semi-final 1–0 to Barnsley in a replay without Fleming at Notts County's ground, after the first game had been drawn 0–0 at Chelsea. The players who will forever be remembered for these glory days, beside Harold Fleming at inside-right, are Len Skiller, Harry Kay, Scots international Jock Walker, Billy Tout, Charlie Bannister, Billy Silto, Bob Jefferson, Fred Wheatcroft, Archie Bown and Jack Lavery. Despite their skills, however, and through no fault of their own, they failed to win Swindon the Football League status that so many people believed they deserved.

A BEVY OF FAIRIES

There was always a bright start to the New Year in St Paul's parish, where the annual two-day carnival held in Milton Road Baths was famous as a bright and spectacular show. In 1911 the *North Wilts Herald* reported:

> There are, as usual, several hundred performers, and there seem to be more groups than ever introduced, with the result that the baths were by no means large enough to comfortably hold the audience and give room for all the performers in the final procession. It was a most interesting spectacle, and presented amid a great blaze of colour, which communicated the greatest possible effect, and gave untiring delight to all concerned. Again no prizes were offered, and everybody entered into the event for the sole love of exacting the fullest possible enjoyment out of it and of helping to assist the object on behalf of which the carnival is being held. This year it is on behalf of the sick of the parish and St Paul's Young Men's Club. Father Christmas with his attendants gave the first flash of colour to the scene, and his entry supplied a seasonable beginning to the merry revel . . . Then came a bevy of fairies . . . and the Kazoo Band . . . in their bright red uniforms caught the musical ear of the audience by their unusual selections. *The Walrus and the Carpenter* was performed by Miss Hoare and Miss Tindley. A number of lads played the part of Red Indians in most entertaining style. The Swindon Town football team (Miss Woodward) was quite a good turn. A skipping song and dance . . . a picturesque presentation of the rainbow, the daisy chain, girls dressed in hunting attire, fairies to interpret a forest group . . . Muscovites in characteristic attire skated round the room to music. Five Little Fags (Miss Dowding) . . . the Polar Expedition, the penguins being almost represented to the life. Irish colleens . . . Grecian dances . . . the costers' honeymoon convulsed the audience with laughter . . . The hunt ball . . . a Swiss group . . . an Oxford and Cambridge boat group . . . Great fun was caused by Swindon Trippers to the Sea . . .

How our forefathers loved dressing up, showing off and making one another laugh – and how willing they were to spend hour after hour at these pursuits. The show outlined above must have taken a considerable period to perform; yet when it was all over, Mr James's Orchestral Band struck up the music and it was time to dance.

But the jollity concealed a darker reality. Hay, straw, coal; the still largely horse-drawn but increasingly mechanised towns of a century ago were entirely dependent on these commodities, and if just one of them ran short, then hardship inevitably followed. Throughout March and into early April 1912 – the spring when the *Titanic* sank – a miners'

strike paralysed the national economy and saw more than a million workers laid off. The railway town of Swindon was obviously not immune to this. The GWR Works was forced into a three-and-a-half day week, the rail timetable was disrupted and, as the movement of freight was regarded as more important than passenger journeys, it became increasingly hard for ordinary people to get around – and for train crews, station staff and shunters to keep their jobs. Fortunately, the town's utilities seemed to hold up, and there was no serious

The children's carnival at the roller-skating rink in the old Corn Exchange early in 1911; lots of light clothes to get dirty on the floor if your skating technique failed you.

threat to gas, electricity or water. It was a chilly spring, however, and the coal merchants found it hard to keep fires burning in every grate. There were even experiments in Swindon into the use of solid oil and coal tar as fuel: a reminder of how resourceful the authorities can be when under pressure. The miners agreed to return to work on 6 April, having made some progress in their demand for wages of 5s per day for men and 2s for boys, but it was some weeks before the wheels of industry and domestic life were rolling sweetly again.

The Empire, scene of Maud Mortimer's great triumph in 1909.

BRUCE'S BOUNTY

The shopping streets of Swindon proved a happy hunting ground for Bruce the dog. He had been collecting for charity since 1905, his money-box strapped to his back, and always gave a woof of thanks as he heard the coins dropped in – but it was his prolific fund-raising in the aftermath of the *Titanic* disaster in 1912 that sealed his reputation as one of the great characters in local life in the years before the First World War. He was well looked after, not just by his owner, Mr Beale of Nelson Street, but by numerous admirers; he won sixteen gold or silver medals for his charitable works, and his collar, too,

was made of silver. The Victoria Hospital was his favourite good cause, though there were many others. They say he travelled more than 10,000 miles on foot and by train to raise some £500 before he died in 1914. Bruce's famous collecting box can still be seen at the museum in Bath Road.

Bruce the charitable dog: the *Titanic* disaster proved his finest hour as a champion fund-raiser.

Into Battle

There is a special poignancy about reports of joyful, innocent occasions on the eve of the First World War, with all its undreamed-of horrors, and all the more so when young military people are involved. The *North Wilts Herald* of 15 April 1913 published a list of some of the gifts presented to Mr Claude Newington, Captain of the 10th Gurkha Rifles, and Miss Constance Evelyn Suzanne Neville on the occasion of their wedding at St Peter's Church, Draycot Park: bride's parents to bride, set of furs; bride's parents to bridegroom, painted miniature of the bride; bridegroom's parents, cheque; officers of the 10th Gurkhas, silver lamp; twelve cheques; brooch; pendant; pearl and amethyst necklace; silver heart-shaped clock; tortoiseshell and silver box; pair of silver candlesticks; enamel and pearl pendant; silver sauce boat; silver tea caddy; lace fan; silver

What lies ahead? A Swindon wedding shortly before the First World War.

tray; silver scent bottle; leather blotting pad; case of fish knives and forks; Irish rug; pair of silver vases; silver hot water jug on stand; gold bracelet; silver box; silver flower pot; pedestal table; cushions; inlaid tortoiseshell-handled paper knife; silver milk jug and sugar basin; silver sugar spoon; silver tea caddy; silver sugar sifter. Let us hope the happy couple lived to enjoy them for many years to come.

AERIAL BATTLES OVER SWINDON

In July 1914, on the eve of war, the *North Wilts Herald* reported that Swindonians were becoming quite accustomed to seeing aeroplanes flying over the town:

> It has become an almost daily occurrence, but on Tuesday the town appeared to be invaded by the aircraft. Speculation was rife as to what it all meant. It now transpires that the machines were engaged in a test. The whole of the available aeroplanes at Netheravon Concentration Camp [*sic*] were engaged in an aerial race to attack an airship. According to the plan, it was reported that a blue airship with disabled engines had been seen drifting somewhere in the area bounded by Cirencester, Fairford, Swindon, Faringdon, Uffington, Minety and Kemble. The airship was represented by a balloon piloted by Major Brabazon. The aircrafts' task was to find this balloon, to circle round it in a left-handed turn, keeping at a distance of not less than a quarter of a mile from it, but near enough to allow the numbers on each aeroplane's rudder to be noted by the pilot of the balloon. The balloon ascended in the morning near Highworth, roughly 50 miles from Netheravon. About 30 aircraft took part in the chase. Promptly at 10am the members of the fleet began to start at intervals of two minutes. The balloon floated at an altitude of over 2,000 feet. Over 75 per cent of the aircraft not only succeeded in finding the balloon, but in encircling it in such close proximity that with guns the 'airship' would unquestionably have been put out of action. There were a few slight mishaps – Major H.R. Brooke-Popham, commander of No. 3 Squadron, had to descend hastily near Cirencester. The machine struck a wall and was wrecked. Major Brooke-Popham was unhurt. Another officer had to come down on uneven ground with the result that his machine was smashed; but again the pilot was unhurt. Monoplanes and biplanes from the Salisbury Plain Flying School were seen over Cricklade, sometimes ten at the same time . . . At about 11am it was noticed that one of the biplanes was descending, and it eventually landed in a field of mowing grass on Mr Hiscock's farm at Oak Barn . . . Mr Hammond soon had a car running from his garage with assistants, and they discovered that the cause of the trouble was a blocked fuel pipe. Fortunately this was soon put right, and the two airmen made a splendid ascent once more and headed back for the Plain.

On 31 July, just five days before war was declared, the headline 'Wiltshire Officer Killed' provided a chilling warning of the horrors to come. In this instance, however, the poor chap had simply fallen off his polo pony in Gibraltar. When the fateful 4 August arrived, ten loud blasts on the GWR Works' hooter signalled the outbreak of war, and it is said that within half an hour the first recruits were lining up for action. They would soon learn the realities of fighting in the twentieth century.

On 14 August, with the war just ten days old, the Mayor of Swindon hit out against hoarders:

. . . people in some cases unwisely and unfairly purchasing food supplies beyond their immediate and usual requirements. It is believed that the practice has not obtained to any very great extent in Swindon, but we should like to urge upon everyone how unfair it would be to their poorer neighbours to purchase more than is absolutely required from week to week. The food supply is ample for everyone, and we hope that all traders in food supplies will, as far as possible, refrain from making any undue increase in prices.

THE HAMMERMAN POET

There was never another Wiltshire poet quite like Alfred Williams, who wrote of his years in the GWR Works in the prose account *Life in a Railway Factory*, published in 1915. Here was a man who knew both town and country at grassroots level, and was able to write equally powerfully about both. He was born in 1877 as the fifth child of a

Alfred Williams, the Hammerman Poet, with his wife Mary. (*Alfred Williams Society*)

family of eight in South Marston, four miles out of town, and his early working life was on the farm; but when he was fifteen he went to work at GWR, first as a rivet hotter, later as a furnace boy and finally as a drop stamper (or hammerman). In his 1915 book he described the culture shock of his change of work, its hardships and the cycling from home daily, in all weathers. In 1914 he gave up work through ill-health, but served as a gunner in the First World War, including a spell in India; he devoted his remaining years to studying, market gardening and tramping the streets of Swindon to scrape a sparse living selling his books door to door. He had patrons in Lord Edmond Fitzmaurice and the Poet Laureate Robert Bridges, who encouraged his raw talent rather as George Bernard Shaw had done with the 'Super Tramp' W.H. Davies; certainly his thirteen books, produced between 1909 and 1931, the year after his death, were published by three leading names in Erskine Macdonald, Duckworth and Basil Blackwell. Williams' real satisfaction, however, was in self-taught scholarship, and it was during his time at GWR that he launched himself into the serious study of English, French, Latin and Greek. After serving in India he studied Sanskrit, produced two books of translated eastern folk tales and called the South Marston cottage he built and shared with his wife Mary 'Ranikhet', after the hill station where he had spent his time in India. For Swindon, though, Williams will forever be the Hammerman Poet, whose work is still commemorated at the Richard Jefferies Museum at Coate, and who touched the town's soul with such lines as:

> Up the furnace door was lifted,
> And the searching glare shot out,
> Lighting up the dusty rafters,
> And the alleys all about.

As the war progressed, stories of deeds of valour began to filter home, and young men who might otherwise have been serving apprenticeships or labouring were returning to Swindon with stories that simply amazed their friends and neighbours. One such was Reg Randall of Taunton Street, for whom the war was an irresistible adventure. At the age of fifteen he had enlisted in the 3rd Wiltshire Regiment but served for only a month before his frantic mother had him sent home again. At sixteen, though, he was off again, this time to the Royal Navy, being assigned to HMS *Warrior* just days before the Battle of Jutland. Again his parents feared the worst, only to be reassured by telegram that he was fine and coming home on leave. Among his souvenirs, when he arrived, were two pieces of shell. Reg told the *North Wilts Herald* that the *Warrior* had sailed to battle with HMS *Black Prince*, *Lion*, *Tiger*, *Defence* and *Edinburgh*:

It was off the coast of Denmark that we sighted the German fleet, turned round and opened fire at 15,800 yards. The *Warrior* was hit about five minutes after it opened fire but it still kept firing until midday. After sinking one ship and setting another on fire we caught fire and had to be towed out of the firing line. We lost a great many men through poison gas from the shells. We tried to get our vessel along, but it was no use, as she was sinking fast, and we had to leave her. A ship which was running about with aeroplanes on it picked us up and brought us to land, and then we went aboard the *Edinburgh*, where we were given cake, bread and butter and tea. Our captain gave us a very good name and is trying to get us on to another ship together. He told us we were one of the best crews he had ever had, and he was more than satisfied with us.

The youthful tar, as the *Herald* dubbed Reg Randall, said he felt lucky to have avoided injury:

I was supplying ammunition for the 7.5-inch gun turret. This was the first action I had been in and it came off greatly, but I still don't want to see any more like it. Of the ship's boys, only one was lost. He was shot as we were leaving the scene of the fight. We were chased by four German destroyers, but some of our destroyers came up and drove them back. As we were leaving our vessel for the one that took us off, a man with a leg off fell between the two ships, but another jumped in after him and fetched him up unconscious. He was brought round, but died on the way to land. One man was left on the *Warrior*. We lost only one officer, the chief carpenter. We had respirators made of cotton tied round our mouths and noses, and it was through this that I was saved from being gassed.

At least some men found work when they came back from the war.

As the war raged on the continent, those left behind fought their own battles. A dispute over how much the Swindon and District Hospital Board should pay a night watchman was sparked off in 1917 by a board member, Reuben George, who claimed that 25s per week plus 5s war bonus was 'not a big wage to attract a man at this moment – do you think we shall get a man who is at all a man at that wage?' The chairman, Mr Bull, retorted that plenty of ratepayers would be happy with 30s a week all-in, but when the clerk revealed that no one had come forward to apply for the job, Mr George proposed that the salary should be raised by 5s. He found no seconder. It was argued that the head gardener earned only 25s plus 5s, and a 'labourer' could not possibly be paid more. Nobody could be found at the workhouse to do the job, and Mr George pricked consciences when he said: 'They are willing to let out a convict from Portland – if you pay him properly.' He also pointed out that a national scheme to attract labourers to the land offered a minimum of 25s plus a rent-free house and a plot of land. How could the board expect to attract a man to town, with its higher living costs, for such a low sum? As was usually the case at such times of impasse, the solution was simple: the matter was referred back to the hospitals' management committee.

As the last German offensive of the First World War began to dwindle in France, Swindon's news was rather less momentous. Nevertheless, the demolition of the Golden Lion bridge (or more accurately bridges) in July 1918 meant a good deal to many people. At the junction of Bridge Street and Regent Street, and taking its name from the pub near by, the GWR-built iron lift bridge was installed to cross the Wilts & Berks Canal in 1870, replacing an earlier wooden swing bridge. Iron bridges with complicated mechanisms were quite a feature of nineteenth-century England, the great transporter bridges of Middlesbrough and Newport being the prime examples. Swindon's bridge, spanning a portion of canal no wider than a lock, was tiny, but local people still admired the Victorian ingenuity that saw it rise to let the barges through. By 1918, however, the needs of road traffic had come to far exceed those of the canal. Next to the lift bridge since 1877 had stood a beautiful and steeply arched footbridge in ornate wrought iron, installed by public subscription to ensure that men from the GWR Works were not delayed when the road bridge was up. It was in 1906 that the last vessel used the Wilts & Berks Canal, and in 1914 Swindon Corporation bought the part of the canal that lay within its boundaries with a view to filling it in for redevelopment. At around that time there were calls for parts of the canal to be retained and developed as a 'Little Venice' and fanciful plans were drawn up by enthusiasts. It was a pity they did not bear fruit; the developers of modern Swindon would have revelled in incorporating a traditional water feature as a contrast to the concrete and glass.

The Inter-war Years

Hundreds of discharged and disabled ex-servicemen demonstrated in Swindon on Sunday 22 June 1919, their peaceful parade accompanied by the Comrades' Band ending in a rally outside the Town Hall. 'We want work, not charity' was their slogan, reflecting a national situation in which more than a million men were jobless, 50 per cent or more of them forces veterans. A vote was passed unanimously for an appeal to the government to introduce factories in which former soldiers and sailors could produce light domestic products. Other demands included women and girls in government work being replaced by ex-servicemen wherever possible, and more generous pensions. The meeting's chairman was that great Swindon champion of the working man, Reuben George, and as usual he pulled no punches. He called on the trade unions to back the ex-servicemen, who were asking not for favours but simply for their just rights: 'If you had been so anxious to see that they got fair treatment as you have been to get better wages for yourselves, these men would not be pleading here this afternoon.' A man who had lost an arm decried as totally inadequate his pension of 27s 6d a week. An old warrior raised cheers when he told the government: 'Instead of passing resolutions for the release of conscientious objectors, why don't you pass a resolution for the release of all soldiers who have done their duty?' He also attacked the level of gratuity paid to lower ranks on leaving the services. After going through five years of agony, it was a disgrace that men should be offered such a miserable sum as £30. The most acrimonious speech, from F.C. Whitby, the regional organiser of the National Federation of Discharged Sailors and Soldiers, was left until last. 'Why not make Germany pay for higher pensions for disabled men?' he asked. 'Furthermore, [the Germans] should be made to repair every bit of damage they have done.' Mr Whitby said that when the men had gone away to war, they had been hailed as heroes, and all sorts of promises were made to them – but the only men who had actually received anything were the profiteers and the men who stayed at home and made fortunes out of the sacrifice and blood of their fellow men. The country had honoured those men by making them dukes and earls (cries of 'Shame'). There were thousands of employers who were sorry that peace was going to be signed. 'And the shopkeepers, too,' agreed a voice in the crowd. Feelings were beginning to run high, and it was obviously time to call it a day – but worse was soon to follow. The Swindon branches of the NUR and ASLEF rail unions went on strike for nine days in the autumn amid growing resentment against the ruling classes, and in July 1919 there occurred the great flagpole incident.

Swindon's very formal and correct war memorial in Regent Circus, clearly modelled on the Whitehall Cenotaph, was unveiled by the mayor, Alderman Samuel Walters, on

The war memorial *in situ* at Regent Circus, after a stormy period in Swindon's history.

30 October 1920. It replaced a temporary wooden one, which in turn had been put up in haste after a 50-ft flagpole erected to mark the peace celebrations of July 1919 had been burned down by crowds incensed by the council having spent £121 on it, while ignoring the plight of struggling ex-servicemen. Even today, £121 for a wooden pole seems steep at a time when many families were surviving on less than that per year; the stone memorial cost £1,125, most of it raised by subscription. In what was as close to a riot as anything Swindon saw in the last century, the men danced and sang around the blazing pole, and later young hooligans ran around breaking windows and looting shops into the early hours. It was easy to blame them for the bulk of the trouble, but in fact it was clearly sparked by disaffected ex-servicemen at a time when the trauma of the First World War was still not far beneath the surface of everyday life. More than a thousand Swindon men died in the war, and for years afterwards grieving relatives strewed the base of the memorial with flowers.

Gradually, however, things got back to normal, and the town's morale received a tremendous boost in 1920 when, after being among the giants of the Southern League for so long, Swindon Town FC were elected into the Football League for the 1920/21 season. So, in truth, was every other club in the Southern League except champions Cardiff City, who stepped straight up into Division Two. The league formed, the Third Division South, lasted until 1957/58, when the two regional Third Divisions were

The Swindon Town team that gained admission to the Football League in 1920. Harold Fleming is second from the left on the front row.

nationalised as Divisions Three and Four. With the lower leagues today in such a precarious state, there is now serious talk of a return to the more inexpensive north–south format, but that was of no concern to the proud Robins players as they trotted out to make their League debut at home to Luton Town on 28 August. In fact, nothing in the world was of any concern to them that day, as they rattled up a 9–1 victory – a score that still stands as the club's League best to this day. There were twenty-two pros on the books for the new challenge, though there was nothing new about Harold Fleming as captain.

The opening match's forward line of Jefferson, Fleming, Rogers, Batty and Davies was exactly the one that played in the club's last Southern League game at home to Southend but, goalkeeper Nash aside, there were big changes in defence. Kay, at right-back, was already on the staff, but he had a new left-back partner in 'Mitts' Macconachie, a late signing from Everton, who even in balmy Swindon liked to wear gloves on chilly days; at least it gave the sartorially conscious fans something other than Harold Fleming's long sleeves to talk about. The brand new half-back line consisted of Langford, from Stalybridge Celtic; Hawley, all but six feet tall and an old pro with experience at Sheffield United and Coventry; and Wareing, another Evertonian in search of regular League action. Goalscorers against Luton were the inevitable Fleming with four, Billy Batty with two, including the first, Jefferson, Bert Davies and an own goal. Davies and centre-forward Dave Rogers were both feeling chipper after touring South Africa in the summer with an FA party. After that sensational start, the Robins never did hit such heights again that season – nor indeed did they escape the Third Division South until it was disbanded in 1958. Those early weeks of League football, however, caused a tremendous stir in the town, despite terrace prices going up to 1*s* for adults and 6*d* for children (or boys, as they were known in those politically incorrect days). The attendance record was broken three times in a month, and when Chelsea visited for an FA Cup fixture, the County Ground was bursting at the seams, with 21,260 people crammed in.

PIPPED BY THE POST

The abolition of Sunday postal collections and deliveries in the provinces caused some Swindon traders to fear that commercial life as they knew it would grind to a halt. To make good a £3.5 million annual deficit, the General Post Office proposed to raise postage charges to bring in an extra £2.5 million and to scrap the Sunday post to save an extra £1 million. One Swindon businessman was scathing in his reaction:

> It's preposterous! It means nothing short of the dislocation of business by the holding up of the weekend mail. Every shop, every factory, every business house, every office looks to the Monday morning's letters for the week's work. If these are to be held up till Tuesday, half a week will be lost before a real start can be made. Surely the trade and commerce of the country are labouring under disadvantage enough without this latest imposition. The Post Office is an archaic institution. I suggest that the business people of Swindon – nay, the whole country – should petition against such an obtuse ruling of the Post Master General. The business of the country won't stand it.

THE BAND LOOKS UP

Sunday evening concerts by the Swindon Town Military Band in the Town Gardens were a sure sign that summer was here. Apart from anything else, for such a lot of people the sabbath really was the single day of rest in the week, and Sunday night offered a last chance for some simple enjoyment before Monday loomed once more. The Town Gardens were famous as one of Swindon's prime spots for Sunday night strolling for groups of unattached young men and women, the weekly 'monkey runs' that were so much a part of life in late Victorian times and the first thirty or so years of the twentieth century. Today, couples get together after meeting in clubs or wine bars; eighty years ago a significant number of Swindon marriages were the result of Sunday evening flirtations in the Town Gardens. It is unlikely that many young people in the park in June 1922 paid much attention to the Swindon Town Military Band, but the *North Wilts Herald*'s music critic was very much on the case, encouraging and chiding in almost equal measure. On Sunday evening, he noted, the band

> actually improved on their own form of a fortnight previously and also presented a most carefully chosen (for the most part) programme. Every seat within the enclosure was occupied, and many were turned away from the entrance gate. The public are now

The bandstand in Town Gardens, scene of dubious musical feats but a handsome survivor. Band concerts are still held in the park on summer Sunday afternoons.

The Art Deco bandstand in the Bowl at Town Gardens, another amenity that has stood the test of time and can still look glamorous on big concert nights.

The rustic bridge at Town Gardens is rustic no more; it is decidedly utilitarian, in fact, these days.

Town Gardens in the rain: the rose-beds have stood the test of time remarkably well.

beginning to realise that we can listen to worthwhile music most Sundays, and the provision of further seats should be immediately considered. It is remarkable to compare this year's concerts with those of last, for the improvement is almost beyond belief. A selection from *Lohengrin* (Wagner) was given adequate treatment. A selection from *The Gondoliers* (Sullivan) was given with necessary vigour. Altogether a most meritorious performance.

He was particularly impressed by the euphonium solo, but noted occasional careless patches; the first cornets were the chief offenders, but the flautist also 'made a number of weak notes'.

FAIR PRICES FOR COTTAGES

Property in Westcott Place and elsewhere changed hands at what were seen as fair prices at a Swindon auction. Three cottages, 66, 66a and 67 Westcott Place, went for £40; nos 69, 71 and 73 sold for £150; no. 78, £130; no. 96, £80; nos 98 and 99, £100; and no. 102, £80. A corner shop and premises at 32 Read Street fetched £260, while there were mixed fortunes for the star lot of the day. Ashford Road post office was withdrawn at £500, but later sold privately for more. It was a hefty sum of money, and for it the purchaser got the freehold of the corner shop, two sitting rooms, a kitchen, a large cellar, four bedrooms, a yard, a two-stall stable, a traphouse and a loft.

DRIVING TRADE FROM THE TOWN

In March 1923 Swindon Chamber of Commerce was growing concerned about the number of prosecutions for road obstruction by cars, and feared that trade would be driven away from town. Captain H.C. Dolphin was fined for leaving a car unattended for twenty-five minutes in Wood Street in Old Town, and was told somewhat pompously by the magistrates' clerk: 'The law in Swindon is the same as that all over the country. The King's Highway is for the King's subjects to pass to and fro. You are not to use it as a garage. If an officer comes in from Chiseldon Camp he can put his car in any hotel yard for sixpence, except on Mondays. There is absolutely no need for people coming into the town to leave their cars in the streets.' A chamber of commerce spokesman said his organisation was not against the police doing their duty, but it had asked the superintendent to instruct his men not to wait until a car had been standing for twenty minutes and then report the driver, but to ask him to move the car after he had been waiting a little. The traders of the town were losing a great deal of business through these prosecutions.

GYPSY PAT'S FAREWELL

Three weeks in the autumn of 1923 were greatly enlivened by an evangelism campaign in the town by the charismatic gypsy Pat Smith. There were enormous crowds at his final services in the big Wesley Church in Faringdon Street, afternoon as well as evening, and when the doors were opened an hour before the first service began there were queues winding all round the building and down one side of the GWR Mechanics' Institute. The evening meeting was even more remarkable, and although the building was filled 'almost

The royal visit in 1924: all was formality itself at the wreath-laying at the war memorial, but the king driving the locomotive was not all it seemed to be.

to suffocation' there were still hundreds of people outside. Gypsy Pat arranged for them to go to the Wesley Schoolrooms, where a further meeting which finished just before midnight was held. During the course of his visit, he had also addressed extra meetings at the Empire Theatre, for which the management had made no charge.

There was a similarly good turnout for the visit of King George V and Queen Mary on 28 April 1924, when the royal party spent the afternoon in the town. They left Windsor by rail and had lunch on the way, leaving the afternoon clear for a variety of duties. Their most high-profile appointment was to lay a wreath at the war memorial. A brief visit to the Town Hall was then followed by an inspection of the recently completed final section of the Victoria Hospital, and the rest of their time was spent at the GWR works, looking in on both the medical facilities and the workshops. There the workers cast a plate of welcome eight feet square or more – an odd piece of folk art which survives to this day. Another piece of folklore surrounded the mile-long journey back from the works to the station. The king, understandably, had a soft spot for the GWR locomotive no. 4082 *Windsor Castle*, and firmly believed he 'drove' it on this short trip. In fact that particular engine was not available on the day, so another Castle class engine was drafted in and adorned with newly cast name and number plates. In those less questioning times, there was no great inquest into the cost of such a gesture.

READING BY NUMBERS

Swindonian Bill Bryant looked back on his 1920s childhood in his later years in a memoir he called *Nobody had Reverence*. He was born into the railway community in 1914 and lived in Jennings Street, Rodbourne, one of the first private housing developments in the area after the GWR estate was built in Victorian times. He recalled just how all-enveloping the railway culture was:

> The person down our street who did not work in the railway factory was an isolated case.
> I can only remember the one or two: Mr Wise in the corner shop, the fish shop, a man who
> used to go round the street with his fish on a truck, the odd baker and roundsman. Other than
> that, everyone used to work in the railway, and there was a closeness and identity with the
> factory . . . the Wises were green with envy at what they considered to be the privileges of
> working in the factory.

He explained that working in the factory meant that for a penny a week there was what today would be seen as cradle-to-grave health care. Bill and his friends also went to the surgery for free liquorice powder, and for Vaseline to use as hair grease, a liniment for football or for smearing on before outdoor swimming. The GWR also operated a lending library – almost certainly before McIlroys started theirs, which was seen by many as the first in town – and Bill and his sister used to dread having to go for books for their mother. She would borrow neighbours' tickets and take out up to six books a week, and it would be left up to them to collect them. Choosing library books was somewhat akin to a present-day Argos shopping experience. You would leaf through catalogues, pick a book, give its number to a woman in a kiosk and wait for it to come out from the depths of the stock-room. There was also the reading room of the Mechanics' Institute, which was open

Dinner time at the GWR Works: what was happening in Swindon was so unlike life elsewhere in this part of the world that endless postcards were published of milling masses of men.

to members' children and justly famous, in Bill's view, for stocking local papers from faraway places with strange-sounding names – well, from Scotland, Ireland and the North East, at least: 'My Uncle David, who was a Scot, always went down there on a Tuesday night to read the *Scotsman* or *Glasgow Herald*. It was a source of reading that was encouraged. I know how excited I was when I was old enough to go in there. I used to spend hours savouring news from the rest of the country.'

Yet in *Nobody had Reverence*, Bill Bryant also considered the flipside of GWR paternalism: the strict hierarchy that kept everybody more or less in their place:

Although my father was so proud of his job, he knew full well that his position in the gradings in the factory was of a low key . . . I think I could not be open to challenge when I say that if you were of a certain grade of an apprenticeship, say a brass moulder, you could not get your children apprenticed to any grade higher than the one above you. You could not get elevated to a fitter and turner, which was one of the highest rankings. You had to stay on that level. There was a scale of what we call differentials today, and however brilliant the boy was, if his father was a moulder then he could only move up one . . . The old establishment imprinted on society the differentials and of course there were differentials in every way from a work point of view . . . A system of inequality was bred into the work force of the town. They were divided by craft, they were divided by wage rates and they were divided by opportunities.

Expectant faces at a children's fête in Edwardian times, and the GWR Park in one of its quieter moments.

Carnival time in Faringdon Road. Hill's the dairymen had a farm in Broome Manor Road.

The General Strike year, 1926, saw forty thousand people flocking to the park for the GWR's annual children's fête, and families picnicked on the lawns of the park in the 'usual glorious weather'. Entry fee was sixpence for adults and threepence for children, though several working men's clubs broke new ground by giving their members' children free tickets. Even those youngsters who paid to get in got a good deal, since their threepence bought them a half-pound slab of cake, a cup of tea and a ride on the switchback or a roundabout. The best trick of all was somehow to avoid being spotted by the attendant, keep your ticket and so get another ride for nothing. The fête opened at half past one, and by four o'clock the three tons of cake had all been consumed, along with forty pounds of tea, three hundredweights of sugar and thirty gallons of milk. On stage in the afternoon a show went on for hours – clowns, jugglers, tumblers, acrobats, comedians and singers all took their turn. Professor Steel's Punch and Judy, Senorita Telma on the trapeze, Kando and Hanako, Japanese jugglers, the Fandor troupe of lady trick-cyclists, the Sisters Austin, tomboy acrobats, the comics Fame and Fortune, Howard and James, the Mezittis – the bill simply stretched on and on, all accompanied by Mr Monk's orchestra. In the evening Trevor Matthews and his orchestra took over the musical duties at a dance at the Drill Hall, while a firework display in the park left the audience gasping and cheering at its patriotic set-pieces, whooping as gradually fading battleships fired rockets at one another, and singing *God Save the King* to the accompaniment of the railway band. All this and late buses, too, with the last services to the surrounding villages not leaving the Centre until quarter to eleven at night.

The aristocratic Fitzroy Pleydell Goddard, the last Lord of the Manor of Swindon, who died in 1927. His family home, The Lawn in Old Town, fared just a little better, surviving until 1952.

The High Street, with the Goddard Arms on the left.

The Goddard Arms today, seen from Wood Street.
Keeping the creeper in trim must have been a steady
job over the years.

Toffish times at the Corn Exchange. The Vale of the White Horse Hunt meets at around the period of Pleydell Goddard's death in 1927.

August 1927 brought the death at the age of seventy-four of the last Lord of the Manor of Swindon, the patrician Fitzroy Pleydell Goddard, who had been born in 1852 and was educated at Christ Church, Oxford. He had been Lord since the death of his father Ambrose Lethbridge Goddard in 1898, and spent his life in the diplomatic service before settling back at the family home, The Lawn in Old Town, where a long-established hotel still bears the Goddard name. He lent his name to several conservative causes; he was a major in the Wiltshire Yeomanry and a leading Freemason; and though he is best remembered now for a photograph showing him in old age with a pet tropical bird on his finger, there is no reason to suppose that he was quite as easy-going and quirky as this picture suggests. Another of his interests was Christ Church, where he was a warden for several years, and even into the 1920s he and his wife Eugenia insisted that the staff at The Lawn should attend Sunday services, at risk of an inquest with the major if they failed to do so. Deeply enmeshed in the charitable and social life of Swindon, he also expected his servants to aid his favourite causes. This was manifested in various ways, the most attractive being the ice-cream they made and sold for the Victoria Hospital annual fête. Major Goddard's funeral was an elaborate affair, though he spurned the family vault at Holy Rood for a place in the burial ground at Christ Church. The Lawn was built in about 1770 on the site of a late medieval manor house, and it was a handsome building in formal grounds that deserved a better fate than demolition in 1952. It was left empty when Mrs Goddard died in 1931, and occupation by American troops in the Second World War all but sealed its fate.

July 1929 saw the last of the trams in Swindon, and the appearance of double-decker buses on the streets for the first time. Nevertheless, though both decks were now enclosed, it would be several more decades before the lower deck ceased to be known as 'inside'. As on the opening day in 1904, tramcar No. 1 played a key rôle in the closing ceremony. Gaily decorated and watched by a big crowd, it travelled the Gorse Hill–Rodbourne route for the last time with members of the electricity and tramways committee aboard. It seems that Alderman W.R. Robins, the committee chairman, kept the atmosphere light with 'a pleasing little speech' at the entrance to the tram shed on Manchester Road, followed by a hearty handshake for George Cathcart, the driver. There was certainly no thought of hanging a wreath over the car, as had become the custom in many towns when the trams made their farewell; in Swindon there was a rather cheerful rush for souvenirs, with Councillor A.P. Scull snatching the last punched ticket, no. NY3290.

Swindon was marching boldly into the future, and another important step was the arrival of talking pictures on 16 September 1929, when the Regent Theatre was opened by the mayor, Councillor J.H. Stevens. This meant the other cinemas of the day, the Central Palace, Palladium, Arcadia and Rink, would soon have to follow suit or die. The first attraction at the Regent was *Bulldog Drummond*, starring Ronald Coleman. The first 'all-talking' picture, it had recently run for fourteen consecutive weeks in London, and was such a big draw on its first night in Swindon that 500 of the 1,800 people wanting to see it had to be turned away. This tale of a young ex-army officer in search of excitement after the war had already been a hit as a novel and a stage play, and it was an obvious choice for early 'talkie' treatment. Sound only extended to the main feature, however. Also on the bill, 'for those who prefer the silent films', there was Alexander and

The Regent cinema at around the time the talkies came in. The fact is advertised on the frontage, suggesting that at least some rivals had yet to catch up.

The Savoy cinema then and now. It is not only
banks that have been turned into wine bars.

Rose in the screen skit *Big Berthas*, which was probably less intriguing than its title, and the British Movietone News. Mr W. Raymond, formerly of the New Gallery Kinema in London, played the two-manual organ supported by Mr J.L. Taylor and Lesley Taff. Normal evening prices were front stalls 6*d*, centre stalls 1*s* and back stalls 1*s* 6*d*, but you paid an extra 6*d* for the centre and back stalls on Saturday nights.

As the school summer holidays approached in 1930, statistics revealed a great mystery: of some 240 women teachers in Swindon schools, the vast majority of them spinsters, only seven per year tended to resign to get married. What was the explanation? The *Evening Advertiser* could hardly believe there was any truth in the traditional picture of the schoolmistress as 'a bespectacled woman with a forbidding countenance', but it did wonder whether Swindon's cautious bachelors were 'afraid that the schoolmarm attitude would be carried into married life, with the unfortunate husband as the pupil, without even the compensation of a long holiday'. Dismissing both thoughts, it concluded that with a good salary and respected social standing, many women teachers would prefer to live in independent comfort rather than giving it all up for 'love in a cottage'. But what it continued to fail to understand was why the men who spent the most time with the schoolmistresses – the schoolmasters – so seldom chose to marry them.

THE GREAT CHRISTMAS EVE FIRE

A fire at the GWR Mechanics' Institute late on Christmas Eve 1930 devastated the main hall and lecture room, while the reading and recreation rooms and library were damaged

by water. The GWR brigade, soon to be joined by the town firemen, fought the blaze for eight hours, and it 'provided a thrill for hundreds of people' as it developed into Swindon's biggest, most destructive fire for years. It wiped out the town's major meeting hall, and the organisers of more than a hundred bookings stretching well into 1931 were left looking for alternative venues. The cause was traced to a fault in an electrical fuse on the stage of the main hall, so there was no blame attached to the last people to use the room, the GWR veterans who had gathered for their annual Christmas share-out. The firemen eventually left the scene at seven o'clock on Christmas morning, and several of them were too exhausted to enjoy their festive dinner until evening.

The GWR Mechanics' Institute in its prime.

Right and opposite left: The Mechanics' Institute again, not after the fire but as it stands today – another case for instant and decisive action.

LIFE ON THE DOLE

With Britain sunk deep in Depression, on 2 October 1931 the *Evening Advertiser* set about discovering how an unemployed Swindon man with a wife and four children managed to keep his family together on 34*s*. The sum was made up of 17*s* a week for himself, 9*s* for his wife and 2*s* for each child under fourteen. 'An unemployed man nowadays is not necessarily a ne'er-do-well', the paper still felt obliged to explain, going on:

> He is quite probably a skilled and conscientious labourer who has had regular work for years and years. In this case he cannot exactly be called a drain on the country's finances, because he is drawing benefit to which his years of regular contributions entitle him . . . Every day he has to trail out in search of work which he knows he will not find. Every day he comes home to days of idleness and pottering around the house, helping the wife and hoping for the best. He is lucky if he has a patch of garden or an allotment to work in. Meanwhile, the wife has the job of balancing the family budget.

In Swindon, that worked out something like this: rent 9*s*; insurance 2*s* 7*d*; coal 1*s*; gas 1*s*; bread 4*d*; tea 9*d*; meat 2*s* 6*d*; bacon 6*d*; sugar 9*d*; margarine 1*s*; vegetables 1*s* 6*d*; jam 5*d*; rice 2*d*; flour 6*d*; eggs 10*d*; currants 2*d*; milk 1*s* 9*d*; soap, matches, firewood, etc. 1*s*; tobacco 9*d*. This all added up to £1 6*s* 6*d*, leaving just a little over for clothes, amusements, newspapers and unexpected expenses.

BURNING ISSUE IN THE WORKHOUSE

At a meeting of the Chippenham workhouse guardians in October 1932 Swindon was blamed for being easy-going on 'casual' visitors to its institution smoking in their ward. It was accepted that permanent residents should be allowed cigarettes and tobacco, but there was much debate in Wiltshire generally about whether the privilege should be extended to overnight residents, who could roughly be divided into tramps or 'roadsters' and men roaming the country looking for work. Colonel L.E. Morrice at Chippenham led the objections to casual visitors lighting up, and against the county-wide Public Assistance Committee's decision to allow it, with the local guardians fixing the permitted hours. 'May I enter another strong protest against the action of the Public Assistance Committee in permitting this smoking against the wishes of most of the guardians' committees,' he said, to murmurings of 'hear, hear'. 'I don't know who are the people responsible for getting them to do this – I believe Swindon is the culprit, chiefly – but certainly most guardians' committees disapprove of it altogether.' The public assistance officer, Mr L. Hussey, agreed that most Wiltshire guardians opposed smoking in the casual wards on fire safety grounds, but added that a standard permitted period of between 8am and 5pm was emerging throughout the country. If Wiltshire workhouses did not follow suit, and insisted on taking away cigarettes on the casuals' admission, they would be 'inviting difficulties with tramps, who sometimes grouped themselves together and formed bands'. Mr Hussey added that the Swindon workhouse manager had found there was no difficulty in taking away the men's smokes after permitted hours. The last word was left to the peppery Colonel Morrice, who listened with increasing impatience as Mr W. Small argued that as smoking was even allowed in prisons these days, it should certainly be permitted for men going around the country looking for work. 'Yes,' replied the Colonel. 'The Government even supplied the tobacco in prisons; if Mr Small was so keen to see it in the workhouse, perhaps he could pay for it too.' This challenge was not discussed further, and instead the Chippenham committee called on the county authority to reconsider the question, and to set the hours itself if it still agreed to permit smoking.

TRIP WEEK

The GWR's annual break for its Swindon workers, universally known as Trip Week by this time, was regarded, locally at least, as the world's biggest excursion. In 1934 employees of the company's Locomotive, Carriage & Wagon Works and their wives and families, totalling 27,416 people, left on Friday 14 July in thirty-one special trains, with orders to report back to work on Monday the 24th. Most of the action happened between 4.50am and 8.05am: in those 3 hours and 15 minutes some 22,248 people boarded twenty-four special trains at the rate of more than 100 per minute and left for 350 seaside resorts in all parts of the country. It was an extraordinary scene. They all wore their Sunday best, with Dad invariably in his white collar and tie, and teenage boys maybe being allowed to settle for school blazers and open-neck shirts. GWR officials, not surprisingly, prided themselves on this great feat of organisation, often achieving the aim of enabling half of Swindon's population to be sent off without the slightest hitch or a minute's delay. Every train was numbered; every passenger was allocated to a train and given full information about the place and time of departure, changing points, and arrival and returning times. That said, it did not always go as smoothly as the GWR publicity machine suggested. For a start, many of the trains had to wait in the sidings, and there was a tremendous scramble to board them from ground level. More to the point, although the travel was free, accommodation at journey's end was not – and it was 1938 before the workers were given holiday pay. Until then, merely being allowed to take a week's break with the company's blessing was seen as enough. The first GWR trip from Swindon was in 1849, when 500 people enjoyed a day out in Oxford. It was not until 1913 that the holiday was extended from a day to a week. 'Savings have been withdrawn, holiday club funds distributed, wardrobes replenished and hundreds of tons of luggage sent in advance,' the *Evening Advertiser* said on the eve of the 1934 trip, forecasting that on the big day families would descend on the station in 'buses, taxis and milk floats'. The favourite resorts that year were: Weymouth, 3,289 adults, 2,203 children; Weston-super-Mare, 2,627 and 1,054; London, 3,142 and 862; and Barry, 1,172 and 860. 'By 8am on Friday, Swindon will be the most deserted town in the country,' the *Advertiser* concluded.

But if the trains ran smoothly, other forms of transport in Swindon were not always plain sailing. Traffic roundabouts have been causing people grief for longer than you might have imagined. In July 1933 Mark Watts of Ferndale Road was ordered to pay 5s at Swindon Police Court for riding the wrong way around the Town Hall. Constable Peare said he saw the defendant pass the traffic signs and when he spoke to him about it he replied: 'I'm sorry. I made a mistake – but I remembered it as soon as I saw you.'

A VISIT TO SWINDON

One reason for a certain snobbish condescension towards Swindon in intellectual circles stems from J.B. Priestley's travelogue *English Journey*, published in 1934. Priestley, with his no-nonsense Yorkshire accent, was widely known through his radio broadcasts as a man of the people, but he spent little time in sparing the feelings of the people of Swindon. He clearly loathed the place. A 'taxi of sorts' took him from the station to a hotel in Old Town, where 'I found the chambermaid busy trying to fasten the wallpaper in my room to the wall with drawing pins', and he was prompted to think that 'if drawing pins could have restored paintwork, I would have sent out for another box'. Venturing down to New Town, he admired the little gardens of the 'tiny semi-detached houses of red brick', and concluded that while there was something 'miniature and monotonous' about these homes, at least some sort of life could be lived in them. The same could not be said for the Victorian railway cottages, where everywhere there were 'the same squat rows. It was like wandering through a town for dingy dolls . . . A number of bees and ants, cynically working in bricks and mortar . . . could not have worked with a more desolating uniformity.' At dinner time at the railway works, he found the men pouring through the gates at the end of a shift: 'a sturdy lot with blackened faces, much too sturdy and far too grimy for the dolls' houses they had to go to.' After that, Priestley progressed to the main street, Regent Street, which was 'a poor thing, chiefly filled with cheap shops and sixpenny bazaars. There were plenty of women going in and out of these shops, for the men of the town were in steady work . . . but you felt that all the shoddiest stuff of Europe, America and Japan were being poured into this street.' He ate a vile lunch in an eating house 'noisy with gramophone music coming from the wireless', and after he had abandoned his 1*s* 3*d* meal in which 'the pork was nearly all dubious fat, the Brussels sprouts were watery and the baked potatoes might have been made of *papier-mâché*', life back on the street would have seemed a good deal brighter had it not started to rain.

Priestley's evening meal back at the hotel proved better than expected, and a dull variety bill at the Playhouse was enlivened by a vibrant little dancing girl who stood out from all the rest of the 'troupe of energetic but ungraceful dolls': 'There are not enough of her kind, whether they are pretending to be golliwogs on the stage or pretending to be real people in the street.' Otherwise, he found the night life of Swindon consisted of the three picture houses, the poor little pubs and the odd fish and chip shop. This, he concluded, was

one of the penalties inflicted upon you if you live in these smaller industrial towns, where you can work but cannot really play. A town in which men have worked hard all day at their giant engines ought to be glittering and gay at night, if only for an hour or two. This street should be ablaze with light. One ought to be able to look through great windows and see the triumphant engine-makers and their wives, sweethearts, children, eating and drinking and dancing and listening to music beneath illuminations as brilliant as their furnaces.

Right and overleaf: Coate Water in its heyday – a place for relaxation, recreation and simply getting away from it all.

A tale of two diving stands. The complex
wooden structure gave way to Art Deco concrete
elegance in the mid-1930s. That structure has
long been redundant but it still stands, an
eyesore to some, a stylish reminder of the past
to others.

Water polo was a great craze in the early years of organised swimming at Coate Water.

But it wasn't all toil and grime for the people of Swindon. The now-redundant Art Deco concrete diving stage at Coate Water was opened in June 1935 by the mayor, Councillor Frederick Hobbs, at a grand diving and swimming gala. The highest board was almost 24 feet above water level. The elegant structure, designed by the borough surveyor with more than a little help from current international trends, replaced a stage of wooden scaffolding which dated from the early years of the century. Coate Water stems from a reservoir built for the Wilts & Berks Canal in 1822, and the 'Lido' craze of the inter-war years saw the swimming side of its attractions develop, alongside boating and occasional skating. A combination of weed, mud and a polio scare in 1958 saw an end to official swimming there, but the diving stage still stands as a reminder of long-ago summers of knitted swimsuits, water polo matches and beauty parades.

In July 1935 it was reported that just one mother had died giving birth in Swindon in the previous year, producing a maternal mortality rate of 1.25 per 1,000 births. This was a quarter of the average rate for the whole country, showing that whatever did or did not happen in the terraces of human 'breeding boxes' at which the intelligentsia sneered, the needs of pregnant women were not neglected.

Also in July that year three uncommon winged insects, each measuring more than an inch long, were caught by an assistant in a Wood Street chemist's shop. They were black and yellow and looked capable of inflicting a sharp sting, and somebody thought they looked suspiciously like the tsetse fly from Africa, whose bite could be fatal to horses, cattle and dogs – and did humans no good, either. Experts dismissed the idea, however, although without disclosing exactly what the insects were.

DEPRESSION? WHAT DEPRESSION?

Swindon's new employment exchange was opened in July 1935 by Colonel A.J. Muirhead MP, Parliamentary Secretary to the Ministry of Labour. It came at a time when the town seemed to be pulling out of the Depression, with 3,870 men having found jobs in the previous eighteen months. The mayor, Councillor Hobbs, even foresaw that, at the current rate, there would be no registered unemployed left at all in two years. 'If that's the case,' replied Colonel Muirhead, 'I'll be happy to return to Swindon to close this employment exchange down.'

More than a thousand children of the unemployed and poor families were entertained to the annual Christmas tea on New Year's Day 1936 at a new venue, the Drill Hall in Swindon. The mayor's only half-joking prediction of no unemployment in the town in two years' time began to look ludicrously over-optimistic when it was discovered that the GWR Mess Rooms, where the treat had been held for many years, simply could not cope with the numbers this time. As with the children's summer fête, the *Evening Advertiser* enjoyed totting up the statistics of the vast quantities of food eaten 'in the space of an hour or so' at what seemed to be miles of tables stretching the length of the Drill Hall. The bill of fare was: 92lb butter, 1cwt (a hundredweight) of sugar, 14lb tea, 320lb fruit, 150lb lardy cakes, 2,000 fancy cakes, 152 loaves, 100 dozen cartons of chocolates, 6 cases of oranges, 2cwt of boiled sweets, 96 dozen packets of biscuits and 7 gallons of milk. Some three thousand paper bags were needed for the food the children took away with them, much of which was doubtless enjoyed at the next day's matinée film show at the Palace, Gorse Hill. There were eighty-five women helpers at the tea, plus forty men and the committee. About £100 was collected in the GWR Works and from various donations, and local churches provided tables and benches. In a message of good cheer for the New Year, Mr W. Wakefield, the town's MP, reminded the children that as there was an extra day to be spent in the leap year of 1936, they should all divide it up so that they spent a few minutes each day in doing a good deed and making the world a better place to live in.

WAUGH AND UNEASY PEACE

In 1937 one of the most unlikely pre-war summit conferences took place as the poet John Betjeman (then a spiky observer of the modernisation of England, rather than the cuddly teddy bear and knighted Poet Laureate he became) explained to the town clerk and borough surveyor why he had been beastly about Swindon. To add piquancy, he took the great intellectual and cultural snob Evelyn Waugh along with him. The cause of the trouble was a radio broadcast in which he had described Swindon as 'floundering about like a helpless octopus, spreading its horrid tentacles out into the quiet village places – a warning to all England to keep clear of the speculative builder . . . People who don't live in Swindon consider it a blot on the earth. The streets are depressing: rows of two-storeyed semi-detached houses packed closely together, and hardly any trees.' The council took such exception to this that it summoned him to explain himself to the town's senior officials. Betjeman, sensing perhaps a lawsuit in the offing, took the matter seriously enough to comply with their wishes – and took a solicitor with him, as well as Waugh. It must be said that Betjeman had an abiding love–hate relationship with the towns of what is now called the M4 corridor. One of his most notorious lines – 'Come friendly bombs and fall on Slough' – outdoes in offensiveness anything he ever wrote about Swindon, but there is great affection in his two-verse tribute to the peal of ten bells at Christ Church in Old Town (give or take the odd reference to 'brick-built breeding boxes of new souls' and the cars changing gear on steep Cricklade Street below).

WHAT GOES AROUND . . .

By the mid-1930s the Town Hall at the top of Regent Street, which had seemed like the centre of the new civic universe when the two town councils merged in 1900, was increasingly regarded as a late Victorian building unequal to the demands of life in the mid-twentieth century. In 1937 new civic offices were begun in Euclid Street, to be occupied fully in the following year – and the civic merry-go-round has taken a few further turns since then.

Rumours of war were already causing alarm in Britain but in October 1938 there were still plenty of people, some of them in very high places indeed, who did not believe that war was inevitable. But in Swindon it all began to feel a great deal more real when the council published its plans for the distribution of civilian respirators or gas masks. It announced that on the instructions of the government to proceed speedily with this, arrangements had been made for the polling stations to be open on the evenings of 4–7 October: 'All residents of the Borough are requested to attend at the Polling Station to which they usually go for voting purposes between the above-mentioned hours for the purpose of being supplied with a respirator.' The council said there were no respirators available for children aged under four – an alarming situation which was apparently still the case a year on, as can be seen from our entry for 1939. Also apparent, already, was the kind of bureaucratic muddle that made many people who lived through those times wonder how Britain ever managed to win the war: 'The Corporation have not yet been supplied with boxes in which respirators can be kept, and all persons are warned to take great care of the respirators, which should be kept in some cool, dry place. Boxes in which householders can keep respirators will be supplied as soon as possible.'

War Once More

The first few months of the Second World War came to be known as the Phoney War, but nobody in town would have believed that in the last days of peace in early September. By the first of the month all the emergency services were on the alert, and the slogan 'Swindon will be ready', intended to reassure, cast an ominous light on what might be in store. All but the most acutely ill patients at the town centre hospitals – the Victoria, the GWR and St Margaret's – were sent home or to outlying cottage hospitals, as the wards were cleared ready for casualties. Offers from blood donors had been flooding in, but it must have terrified some to read that 'in view of the serious turn of events, more are still required'. By the end of 1 September, anyone who had still not been given a gas mask was asked to go to their nearest warden without delay, so it was not surprising that some mothers of babies were frantic when they heard that, even at this late hour, helmets and respirators for little ones had yet to be received in the town. Workmen were spending sixteen hours a day putting up shelters all over the area, and would have put in more hours if the buildings' pre-cast sections had not been in short supply. In view of all this the other big local news of the days leading up to war seemed almost absurd – trains full of evacuees pouring in, packed with unaccompanied children or mothers and babies from London. Later they would come from Hastings, when that vulnerable coastal town came under fire. It is hard to reconcile the two outlooks: one of the south of England's key railway junctions preparing for war as if every day could be the last for many of its residents, while at the same time welcoming thousands of evacuees seeking refuge. In the event, and on balance, those who believed Swindon would provide relatively safe shelter were probably correct. By the end of the war some 104 bombs had fallen on the town, with 48 people killed and 105 injured. Around 50 houses were destroyed and 1,852 damaged to some degree. As for the refugees, 4,254 arrived in anticipation of the war, while at one time 12,000 were expected; but by 10 October, with life apparently going on as in peacetime, more than 1,300 had gone back home to their loved ones in London. No one will ever know how many of them fell victim to the blitz of 1940.

On 2 September the *Evening Advertiser* noted that wellwishers were urged to stay away from the reception centres for the 'little guests', and praised the evacuees: 'Everyone was impressed by the excellent behaviour and cheerfulness of the children. Even at the end of the day, when they were getting tired, the youngsters were still smiling.' At the same time the women of Swindon, who had been 'entrusted a mighty and responsible task', were warned of the young evacuees that 'their standards of conduct, cleanliness and character may not be the same as those on which you have based the education of your own kiddies'; and by the new year of 1940 there was little bright-eyed idealism in the warning that 'if evacuees damage your furniture, you can claim compensation'.

As a footnote, there was an odd little vignette on the afternoon of Saturday 2 September when St Mark's Church welcomed as the opener of its garden fête John Betjeman, whose scathing verdict on the architecture of Swindon will be recalled. Of course he had been invited exactly *because* of the controversy – and equally predictably he was charm and grace itself. He said the organisers' courage and pluck in holding the event in such circumstances typified the spirit of Swindon people, overcoming difficulties that might have proved insuperable to others. It was the kind of day on which nobody was going to get very worked up about an arty youngish man's views on helpless octopi and blots on the earth.

War Weapons Week in Swindon, 9–16 November 1940, was a big hit – but that could be read two ways. Was it mere coincidence that just days later the town that had rallied around a huge poster bearing the slogan 'Lend To Attack Industrial Berlin' suffered its worst air raid to date? The Week's aim was to collect £200,000 to supply bombs and bombers for the Berlin offensive, but with strong business backing the final figure raised was £349,154. As the Swindon population at that time totalled some 61,000, that was seen as a pretty impressive effort. Various fund-raising efforts paid off. There was an exhibition in the town hall, a military band and a meeting addressed by Captain Harold Balfour, the Under-Secretary of State for Air. A German Dornier bomber, sleek and slender and disturbingly beautiful, was put on show in the Town Hall car park. And in another public meeting, held at the Playhouse, the MP for Frome, Mrs Mavis Tate, was cheered to the rafters when she shouted: 'Bomb them to smithereens.' Unhappily, that was the fate of several houses in the Beatrice Street, Ipswich Street and Whitehouse Road area when eight bombs fell there on the evening of 19 November. A Beatrice Street woman died of her injuries, and several evacuees were among many who had lucky escapes.

In June 1941 the Wiltshire Agricultural Education Committee called for a new emphasis on horticulture and food production in schools, both by helping nearby farmers and by starting their own production. A meeting was called with teachers in Swindon to discuss planting potatoes on a 20-acre plot, and it was hoped that a demonstration of what was possible in the town would encourage rural schools in the county to follow suit. The committee chairman, Mr Prichard, hoped schools would cooperate with farmers in the harvest, and he was keen to see a properly planned scheme brought in for elementary schools to help with labour at this vital time, and maybe at planting time, too. There was a certain irony about all this. Schools in rural areas and on Swindon's fringes had traditionally seen absenteeism soar at harvest time, as all hands were called in to help in the fields, and here was the education committee all but building the practice into the curriculum. In any event, Mr Prichard conceded, whether or not there was any formal scheme drawn up this year, the call-up of agricultural workers meant that the committee 'would have to stretch a few points' when it came to its policy at harvest time. 'Turning a blind eye' might have been a more accurate phrase.

Rail traffic in Swindon rose dramatically in the wartime years, and not only because of the huge influx of American and other servicemen. As never before, the station was becoming a distribution point for vast stocks of foodstuffs, and the allotments that were springing up in flower gardens and public parks were only the tip of the iceberg. In July 1941 figures were released about the acreage of grassland ploughed up in Wiltshire during the war. For the 1940 harvest the figure had been 40,000 acres; a further 40,000 would be cultivated in the current year, and there would be a similar increase in 1942. There had been such destruction in Europe, as well as to the vital food convoys, that it was clear that food would be scarce for several years to come. There were reports that the numbers of rabbits had decreased enormously, and naturalists fretted over the effect of this massive upheaval on the Downs' rare butterflies and flora; most of them, that said, kept their counsel, knowing all too well that 'there was a war on'. Soldiers who had been farm workers in civilian life were given permission for a month's leave to help get in the harvest, and the education committee's deliberations of the previous month had borne fruit. The school holidays were arranged conveniently for the harvest, and there were various camps for schoolboy helpers, with the promise of hard work but a bit of fun, too. As well as all this, some fifty road men had been released by the county's road and bridges committee to help on the farms. Wiltshire would not be a county where the grain would rot on the stem for want of harvesters.

THE WORKSHOP WOMEN

Women had long been employed at the GWR Works, and not only in the offices. Since the making of locomotives and rolling stock in the early years of the century presupposed that every last component should be made on the spot, there was never any shortage of women working in the upholstery shop or creating luggage-rack nets strong enough to support naughty schoolboys who would climb up into them on long, boring journeys. It was in the Second World War, however, that the heavy tasks were taken on by women for the first time, with jobs such as blacksmithing, boilermaking and so on. Not only were they replacing the men who had been drafted into the services, but they were helping the war effort directly by turning their hands to producing shell and bomb cases, tanks,

Women tackled work right across the spectrum at the GWR Works in wartime.

landing craft and midget submarines. So many preconceptions were swept aside as the pre-war situation in which women were expected to give up work when they married became one in which marital status was entirely irrelevant – and many women were all too reluctant to give up the camaraderie and steady money of the workshops when the men did eventually start coming home. What happened at the GWR Works at Swindon was typical of the situation at large engineering factories all over the country – but that made the tensions, frustrations and snatched-away freedoms of many workshop women no less easy to bear in the early postwar years.

But war work was not the only challenge Swindon's women faced during the war. Food shortages were causing terrible difficulties but then the *Evening Advertiser* came up with some scrummy suggestions for packed lunches for a whole week. 'You don't want to give them the same old thing every day, and it's not good for them, either,' the women's editor warned. 'People do best on variety, and they need a balance of body-building, energy-giving food, including plenty of protective food, especially greenstuff.' What she had in mind was something like: Monday: sandwiches filled with a mixture of cold mashed potato, grated cheese, chutney and chopped fresh parsley, accompanied by lettuce and followed by a jam turnover. Tuesday: turnover filled with a mixture of chopped cooked beans, melted cheese and chopped parsley, accompanied by a tomato and raw cabbage salad from a screw-top jar and followed by chocolate pin-wheels. Wednesday: potato scones filled with scrambled dried egg, cooked mixed veg and chopped parsley, accompanied by watercress and followed by prune dumplings. Thursday: rissoles made with cooked meat, cooked beans and mashed potato, accompanied by raw spinach and lettuce and followed by fruit turnovers. Friday: soup, followed by sandwiches filled with scrambled dried eggs, mashed potato and chopped fried bacon, accompanied by radishes or tomatoes and lettuce. Saturday: turnover filled with sausage meat, cooked dried peas, herbs, parsley, chopped leek and onion, accompanied by raw cabbage in a screw-top jar and followed by oatmeal scones and jam. And that was the week's fare. It is often said that the diet of wartime Britain was in general far more healthy than today's. On the evidence of that menu it could well be true – but you certainly needed to be healthy in the first place to face up to it.

There were American troops in and around Swindon from 1942 to 1945, and one local girl who welcomed the news was Peter and Mary Fluck's daughter, who grew up to be Diana Dors. She was born in the Haven nursing home in Kent Road in October 1931, which made her not yet thirteen in the summer of 1944. But she was already into wearing lipstick and lightening her hair – 'It's Veronica Lake!' the truckloads of GIs would shout as this precocious child slinked by – and when she and her mother were given the chance to go to a party with a group of GIs at a local hotel, they both jumped at the chance. Mum was keen to get to know the camp cook, and returned home with a bag full of sugar, butter and eggs. As for Diana, she danced every dance, and as all the boys believed her when she told them she was seventeen, she went home thinking she really had grown up. More parties followed, accompanied by the usual kind of scrapes involving spiked drinks and pushy Americans. It was in 1945, in the last few months of the GIs' stay, that the now fourteen-year-old Diana came third in the bathing beauty contest at Weston-super-Mare which became part of the Dors legend. Back home in Swindon one of the GIs' education officers saw her picture in the papers and invited her to bring her swimsuit along and model for the men. She

A beauty contest at Weston-super-Mare helped propel a young Diana Dors (right) towards her chosen career.

was as good as the models in the American film magazines, he told her, and that helped push her along the career path she had always dreamed of pursuing. It meant she was London-bound – but not before one last summer in an increasingly dull and grey-seeming Swindon, during which one of her circle of friends was Desmond Carrington, a Swindonian who would also hit the heights, though in a very different sphere. The last time Diana was known to have been in Swindon was in August 1983, when she opened a Home and Leisure Exhibition at South Marston. She told a few unprintable jokes and said it was always a pleasure to be invited back to Swindon – 'a place I always think about when I'm in other parts of the world'. That remark struck many in the audience as deliciously double-edged. After all, at this very second there must be Swindonians in other parts of the world, lying on beaches, skiing down mountains, sailing on blue lagoons. No doubt they will spare the odd thought for those of us here at home – but will they necessarily be pangs of deep longing to be back in Swindon?

The war finally came to an end in May 1945, and celebrations began in Swindon almost immediately. On 8 May, even before Field Marshal Keitel had signed Germany's final act of capitulation in Berlin, the town had transformed itself 'as if by magic', and 'nearly every street in the town was a triumphant Victory avenue', according to the *Evening Advertiser*. 'Every other bicycle sported a Union Jack, and their riders often had jaunty paper hats. Children in red, white and blue costumes danced in the streets to welcome the peace they had never known.' Individual areas came in for special praise: Rodbourne Cheney, Albion Street, Avening Street, Westcott Place, Norton Grove, Harding Street . . . Bunting, flags, balloons, the painted V-signs that were to be seen in some parts of town for another twenty years or more: the streets were bedecked with them, and the celebrations went on well into the next morning. There had not been time to organise any official celebrations but the mayor and mayoress, Alderman Charles Macpherson and his wife Phyllis, spent the day touring the street parties and were greeted like heroes by the children, who somehow saw them as representatives of the king and queen. In Hillside Avenue the prize for the first three home in the ladies' races was a kiss from Alderman Macpherson. There was a hastily arranged free dance at the Playhouse, which was packed to the limit and raised £30 for an injured servicemen's charity; there was another party at East Street Co-op hall, and a thousand worshippers attended an evening thanksgiving service at Christ Church. The pubs stayed open for an extra hour, and the licensing committee's gesture was 'fully appreciated without being abused'. Appreciated just as much was the return to night-time illumination, with revellers basking in the glow of neon, floodlighting and bonfires and delighted to see the symbolic relighting of the clocks at the Town Hall and Christ Church. Many of the bonfires burned effigies of Hitler, notably in Little London, where the crowd sang *Roll out the Barrel* as the Führer burned, at the Down View Road and Leamington Grove celebrations and in many other places. In a street off Grove Road 'Hitler' was hung from a lamppost, and passers-by paid a penny a time to kick him. For most people, though, revenge came a very poor second to relief and joy.

Dancing in the street in Farnsby Street on VE-Day in 1945. It is hardly a scene of boundless joy, but it was simply good to be alive and free.

The Slow Recovery

The GWR Trip in July 1946 was an austerity holiday in many ways, but most of the Works' 18,000 employees and their families took advantage of what for many of them was their first real holiday since 1939. It was historic in another way, too, as for the first time GWR had granted two weeks' holiday with pay. While the special holiday trains before the war had left Swindon on the Thursday night or Friday morning, the 1946 exodus did not begin until lunchtime on Saturday. In all, twenty-seven specials were run during the weekend, while many people travelled by the ordinary services. More to the point, many of them came back on the ordinary services after a week. Two weeks' paid leave was all very well, but it was a great deal easier on the pocket to spend at least some of the time at home, either going on day trips or simply catching up with gardening or decorating. Four out of five trippers went away for a week or a fortnight, but eight special day-trip returns were run on the following Monday and Tuesday, to Paddington, Weston-super-Mare and Weymouth. As always, the south-west of England was the most popular destination, with 5,375 people heading in that direction over the weekend, and on the Saturday at least the trippers got off to a sunny start.

One of the first television sets in Swindon belonged to Austin Tarrant, an electrical engineer from Whitworth Road, who somehow managed to receive the transmissions from Alexandra Palace, some 70 miles away. Since the Palace's service area was meant to extend no further than a 40-mile radius, this was quite an impressive feat. Early in January 1947 a group settled around Austin's set to watch a variety show which featured the Swindon illusionist Horace King and his wife Betty. Reception was not great, but neither did the viewers expect it to be in the circumstances. Occasionally the picture faded, or dissolved into nightmarish shapes. When the occasional car drove past, the screen was reduced to myriad rows of dancing bright lights chasing madly up and down. The over-riding emotion, though, was one of marvel, that these events taking place all of 70 miles away should be seen simultaneously in suburban Swindon. Over and above that, by happy chance, the screen was never clearer than when Horace King was weaving his magic spells; but the viewers that night left Austin Tarrant's home in the firm belief that the real magician was the man who had invented that amazing box of tricks in the corner of his sitting room!

The early spring of 1947 brought one of the century's harshest spells of weather, but Swindon fared a great deal better than many other communities. Its worst snap was around 5–6 March, when blizzards and swirling winds closed roads out of town in all directions and caused snowdrifts as much as 18 feet deep up into the Cotswolds.

Cottages there were buried, as were cars all over the region in their hundreds. But perhaps the most impressive statistic to come out of those terrible nights is the fact that the council was able to get twenty lorries on to the road to clear the snow – and no fewer than 250 men.

Britain's railways passed quietly into state control on 1 January 1948, for there was no public ceremony to mark the handover of the Great Western and other regional systems to the British Transport Commission. The permanent way programme for the new Western Region of British Railways in 1948 was drawn up to include part of the two years' arrears in maintenance work. The plan was to bring maintenance work completely up to date in the next five years, with 490 miles of track relaid, rerailed or resleepered at a cost of about £3 million. There *was* a celebration in No. 4 Shop at the Carriage and Wagon Works, where a large gathering of trade unionists passed the resolution: 'Calling all workers: in celebration of the national ownership of the railways, we pledge our support in unanimous action to speed production in support of, and to ensure the success of, the British national railways.' The struggles of the pioneers of the trade union movement were then recounted, down to the winning of present-day freedoms and privileges, and the event's significance was underlined by the fact that leading officials of the National Union of Vehicle Builders were present.

By July 1949 there had been no rain for weeks and Wiltshire's farmers were complaining that they were in the depths of a full-scale drought – but Swindon's ice carnival took place nevertheless. That said, it was touch and go, and at one point it looked as if the show would have to be abandoned, as had been a previous attempt to stage an ice show in Swindon. The problem was that the show's equipment all used a DC electricity supply, while the supply in Swindon was AC. A search over a wide area failed to find a converter, and machinery sent down from London also proved unsuitable. This time, though, the authorities offered to put in a new DC cable, and electrical engineers sweated in the afternoon heat to lay it, while other men were assembling a 17-foot square tank which weighed 5 tons. The ice, up to 2 inches deep, took 24 hours to freeze. To start off, 6 hundredweight of ice bought from local sources was spread over the rink, which was then flooded and frozen. Each evening it was so cut up by the skaters that the surface had to be scraped, reflooded and frozen. It came as no surprise to Swindonians, given the topsy-turvy nature of the whole venture, that the reflooding was done with boiling water, which freezes more quickly than cold. Why yes, of course . . .

A curious result of the prolonged spell of hot weather that year was an alarming increase in the number of burst water pipes. From April to July there were 3,224 complaints – though the children revelled in the cooling fountains squirting the streets. Much of the town is built on clay, which contracted in the heat and subjected the pipes embedded in it to all sorts of new stresses and strains. Not that the authorities appeared to be very sympathetic towards their suffering ratepayers, suggesting that they should seek help from local plumbers. 'Many people seem to be under the impression that they must come to the council to have the repairs done,' said a spokesman. 'We have to charge for repairs just like any private firm. We're overloaded, and would like to see the load spread a bit.'

Princess Elizabeth inspecting Boy Scouts on her visit to Swindon in 1950. War wounds were still fresh, and it was not the most relaxed of visits.

A ROYAL VISIT

On 15 November 1950 Princess Elizabeth came to Swindon. The date was significant, as it was very nearly the 50th anniversary of the founding of the borough – a reminder of just how much Swindon and English society in general were rooted in the past. At this stage of our history this had much to do with the aftermath of the Second World War, both in depriving the country of money to make progress and in making us, for a few years at least, crave 'normality' rather than pursuing change. The princess, then a lively young woman of twenty-four, named a locomotive after herself, Star class no. 4057 *The Princess Elizabeth*, and unveiled the name plate of the last Castle class engine to be built, no. 7037 *Swindon*. She also visited and declared open the Garden of Remembrance, and met relatives of victims of the two world wars, all the time surrounded by an entourage of middle-aged and elderly men. Within eighteen months she would be queen, and that sea-change really did shake Britain into re-examining itself and its way forward in life. That

Swindon in the middle years of the twentieth century was a town very different from today's.

was for the future, however; in 1950 the princess's visit was conducted in an old-fashioned way – just as that of her grandparents had been in 1924.

The centenary of Christ Church in Old Town, Swindon's parish church, was marked in 1951 with gatherings and celebrations but also by the most extensive and expensive renovations since 'the Old Lady on the Hill' was built. These included repairs to the organ, major work on the roof and wiring and the removal of seventeen old elms from the churchyard. The vicar, Canon John Gilbert, was nearing the end of his long ministry, and his centenary message was a masterful combination of the rhapsodic and the hard-headed. He said that what the church building meant to the congregation was hard to express:

> We can imagine the loss, were it taken away. Let us be grateful for all the past, as we face the future. The Old Lady still stands waiting expectantly. We had prepared her birthday present in the form of practically a new organ, at a cost of £2,500. It now appears that her old roof must receive extensive repairs. She points to other defects in her wardrobe which will cost some £2,000 to renew. She is confident in the generosity of her children . . .

Earlier, Canon Gilbert had wondered why this, the 100th anniversary, had been the first of the Old Lady's to be marked in any style:

> She has made no complaint, but one can imagine her musing why her birthday has not been observed previously by the people of the town and country, who from 20 miles distant have taken her tapering finger and brooding beauty for granted. With the wisdom . . . generated by age, she smiles with the reflection that only the essentials are taken for granted. In the silent night the moon and the stars, over generations, have shared with her that reflection, no less than the sun in his noonday might . . .

More prosaically, the heart of Regent Street shopping in the 1950s was the central stretch with McIlroys on one side and Woolworth's on the other. Even in 1952 both smacked of shopping in the pre-war years, Woolworth's with its round lamps and polished wood counters and floors and McIlroys with, well, everything really . . . Other familiar names clung around them, paying the highest rates in town in the knowledge that every Saturday tens of thousands of people would be passing their windows. Close to McIlroys stood The Spot, a cycle and sports shop with a small frontage but a huge stock, and between the two was Mac Fisheries, part of a chain founded in 1921 which put a fresh fish shop at the heart of every decent-sized town in the country. They always appeared clean and well-connected. The chain was the brainchild of the philanthropic soap-maker Lord Leverhulme, who saw it as a means of bringing work to remote Scottish communities. The chain met its end in the late 1970s, but for a decade or more afterwards, when shoppers were interviewed about their local high street, the need for 'a good fish shop' always came through as a high priority – it was a pity they did not feel that way when they were abandoning Mac Fisheries in droves for the delights of fish fingers and crispy cod fries. Along from Woolworth's, the jewellers James Walker advertised themselves as the 'diamond ring specialists'; in fact they sold all sorts, but that tag put them at the forefront of every young woman's mind when it came to buying an engagement ring – the most expensive piece of jewellery in most households of the time. Furniture stores were also to be found at the core of the shopping area, including Woodhouse (in the W.W. Hunter building where the Envy clothes shop is now) and Courts, a chain that has since moved wholeheartedly into out-of-town shopping. Morse's small department store, Keogh's hardware shop and Holmes & Lucas's radio shop were also strong names locally, but all the big chains were in Swindon too and as the 1950s progressed it tended to be their shiny frontages and corporate logos that set the trend for the future, with Stead & Simpson, Tru-Form and Bata for shoes, Jax for women's fashions, and Burton's and Weaver to Wearer for men's suits – which by this time were climbing away from the £2 10s or 'fifty shilling' suits that tailors used to promote with such vigour.

Coronation day was 2 June 1953 – so it need hardly be said that it was cold and wet for the scores of street parties and community events which followed that most famous shared experience in British history – the gathering round television sets for a first glimpse of not only a new queen but a new medium. The mayor had a busy day. On VE-Day itself the mayoral tour of street parties had been spontaneous and arranged as it went along, but a great deal of thought was put into this one, in which he was received cheerfully but with none of the near-adulation enjoyed by his predecessor in 1945. Alderman and Mrs Gardner's day began at Christ Church Hall in Old Town at 10am, where they found the Old Headlandians' Orchestra already playing patriotic selections. The mayor declared the Christ Church celebrations open and left a packed hall to watch the television coverage, which began at 10.15am, on no fewer than fourteen tiny-screened sets. The parishioners' get-together continued in the evening, with 'a most appetising' high tea and a carnival of games and dancing, interrupted at 9pm to listen to and then cheer a speech by the new monarch. The mayor, on the other hand, had a busy schedule all day, and between 2 and 7.30pm he went to crown the 'twin' queens at Gorse Hill Rec; to have char and wads at the Marsh Farm Naafi canteen, and enjoy various

Shiny shop fascias are beginning to make their mark at the Centre, the junction of Regent and Bridge Streets. Woolworth's was happy to retain its more traditional look, which served its purpose in almost every high street in the land.

The W.W. Hunter building: occupiers come and go, but Swindonians will never be allowed to forget the business that first traded here.

other Marsh Farm delights; to visit successive parties at the Eastcott Hotel, Broad Street, where he cut the coronation cake, Oxford Street and London Street, the Civil Defence HQ, Gilbert Street School, where he judged the fancy dress, Drove Road Secondary Modern, College Street School, Groundwell Road Catholic School and Immanuel Church Hall. Finally he made his way to the Park and Drill Hall, where he presented National Savings cards and stamps to the children.

Many other stories flooded in on that rainy afternoon. There was a 21-gun salute at the Swindon Sea Cadets HQ; at Kingsdown Rec at Stratton, Lady Godiva found the chill wind more trying than Peeping Toms at an event which attracted 5,000 people and lasted nearly twelve hours; in Prince's Street eight-year-old coronation queen Sheila Barker was taken ill with measles during the morning, so Mary Page, also eight, deputised for her; and people from miles around flocked to Mr and Mrs Poynter's house in Vilett Street. They had decorated it rather in the way that some people go overboard with Christmas lights today. The front of their house was completely covered by a cinema screen decorated with shields and the royal cipher and surmounted by fluttering flags and bunting. It formed

Argyle Street children enjoy the coronation celebrations of 1953.

the background to a statue representing the queen on a base fastened to the wall, dressed in the Poynters' niece's wedding dress and with a cloak made out of a white bedspread dyed blue. A mat made out of hundreds of paper flowers spelled out 'God Save The Queen' in white lettering on a red background with a blue border. At night coloured lighting and a floodlamp illuminated this astonishing scene, and music for dancing in the street sounded out from a loudspeaker in the bedroom. At the 1937 coronation Mr and Mrs Poynter won a prize for the best-decorated house in Swindon, but there seems to be no record of their repeating that success in 1952, despite their tremendous efforts!

Other celebrations marked the days around the coronation. Sir Noel Arkell, the Sheriff of Wiltshire, opened Queen's Park as a permanent reminder of this happy time, and described it as 'the jewel in Swindon's crown . . . It is the country that most of us go out miles to see at weekends . . . Easily the most lovely thing in Swindon.' Meanwhile, at the Gaumont cinema, formerly the Regent, local man Mr E.P. Wyeth was combining his great passion with a dash of patriotic fervour by displaying an assortment of clocks in fifteen different shapes and sizes, including some skeleton models, all of them made in Swindon by the Garrard Engineering & Manufacturing Company Ltd. Also on show was a cheque printer and its components, made by the Westinghouse Garrard Ticket Machine Co., plus Garrard radiogram units, gramophone components and automatic record changers – the gadget for which the company had become a household name by the end of the 1950s, after big heavy plastic 78rpm single records had given way to resilient little vinyl 45s. For a few brief years it was a serious social gaffe among the nation's teens and twenties not to have a record player with a Garrard auto-change. And what did all this have to do with the queen being crowned at Westminster Abbey? Ah, it was there to show off British and Swindonian achievements in the coronation year, you see.

By the mid-1950s, despite the advent of television, cinemas in the town were still flourishing. But in October 1954 the council decided that children aged under fifteen should only be allowed into the town's cinemas on Sundays if they were accompanied by a parent or 'bona fide adult guardian'. There was an objection from Mrs J. Robinson, who said: 'Because there are so many commercial distractions today the unit of the home, the most important unit of our national life, is being seriously undermined, and this must soon adversely affect the nation. As to the "bona fide guardian", I fear we shall see children hanging around cinemas waiting hopefully for someone to whom they can attach themselves. This in itself is a grave potential source of danger to the child.'

Some interesting statistics emerged from a sociological survey of the Swindon district in 1955. About 97 per cent of households owned a 'wireless set' and the other 3 per cent were thinking of acquiring one. On the other hand, only 29 per cent owned televisions, with 16 per cent more saying they were hoping to get one soon; obviously it was a boom market, but a useful reminder that the great rush to buy sets for the coronation of 1953 still had an impact on only a minority of homes. Some 41 per cent owned vacuum cleaners, 11 per cent electric washing machines, just 7 per cent fridges, 6 per cent motorbikes and 60 per cent pushbikes. Cars? – a remarkably high 21 per cent, although there would certainly have been wide areas of inner Swindon where car ownership was nothing like one in five houses. Statistics for the town itself showed that around two-thirds of households had a weekly income of between £7.10 and £12.10, with only 2 per cent bringing in £17.10 or more a week. Six out of ten heads of household were factory or manual workers, 20 per cent clerical, shop or non-manual, and only 8 per cent professional, managerial or executive. Around 11 per cent were retired.

Certainly many of the town's residents felt strongly about their town. In October 1955 a reader's letter in the *Evening Advertiser* praised the town's charms:

> From time to time one reads or hears remarks concerning Swindon's less desirable aspects which would give a stranger the impression it was a town devoid of beauty. . . . This is not so. Some superior persons attempt to ridicule the architecture of our Town Hall, but . . . there are many town halls and other public buildings in the land which by comparison make ours appear handsome. Then what of its delightful little attached gardens and the lovely group of lime trees at the rear? What pleasant shade and interesting rest these trees have afforded to thousands throughout this warm summer. As for Swindon's Town Gardens, a widely travelled man once said to me: 'There is hardly another town which can excel their delightfulness.' Then what of the increasingly beautiful Garden of Remembrance and the Queen's Park, with its idyllic lake? I have been urged to write this letter by seeing the illuminations there . . . Never have I seen such a happy combination of natural and aided beauty: the whole place became a thing of sheer enchantment. If this goes on developing, I can see special train and bus excursions running to Swindon instead of Blackpool to see the illuminations. The fact that this was all free will enable me to pay my rates next time with a lighter heart.

One wonders what Sir John Betjeman would have thought.

The mid-1950s were a strange period: years when a new England, a new world, in fact, was nudging hard up against the old. A decade after the end of the Second World War it seemed that little could be taken for granted any more. Britain tried to act as a traditional colonial superpower in Egypt, and the Suez disaster was the result. No woman was hanged in Britain after Ruth Ellis in July 1955, and in the United States Dr Martin Luther King's black civil rights movement was at last beginning to prick the conscience of the Republican party. On a lighter note, 1956 brought Elvis Presley to the States and teddy boys to Swindon (and to every other British town of any size). Enter into all this the Wiltshire quarter sessions chairman Sir Charles Chitham. He played no rôle in moulding national opinion, but on a local level his words and actions seemed somehow to sum up a society on the cusp of change. The way he spoke to the young wrongdoers up before him was strictly of the old school. One gains the impression he would have clipped them round the ear, given the chance. Yet the sentences he handed down would have struck earlier generations as the almost scandalously lenient product of an over-liberal new age. In July 1956 two young Swindon men, a merchant seaman aged twenty-two and an apprentice fitter aged twenty, were each given a conditional discharge with £5 5s costs after pleading guilty to breaking and entering the house of a Swindon magistrate, Mr Herbert Vaughan Slade, and stealing a gold bracelet, wrist watch, desk lighter, alarm clock, electric razor, five bottles of spirits, a safe, an attaché case, twenty cigarettes and £8 in cash. They asked for two other offences to be taken into consideration. The only explanation forthcoming was that one of the men had been drinking, and did not really think about what he was doing. Sir Charles commented: 'To commit three burglaries in this way seems extraordinary. I could have understood it if it had been only one.' He fined two men charged with breaking and entering Plessey's sports and social club £20 each after they had pleaded guilty, with two months to pay. One man said he had been working late and had been drinking, but could offer no reason for 'such a silly offence'. Sir Charles concluded: 'It is difficult to understand why you did this.' Then, as they were stepping down, he shouted after them: 'And for goodness' sake, don't be such silly fools again!'

These were golden years for the Swindon Robins speedway club, which was formed in 1949 and within a few months was racing in the Third Division of the National League. In 1956 they were champions of the seven-team Second Division – and the following year they went one better, winning the National League championships by a single point from Belle Vue Aces, the crack Manchester club. But 1957 was a sad year for speedway, if not for Swindon. Wembley, Poole, Birmingham and temporarily Bradford ceased operating in the First Division, leading to the Second Division being combined with the First for an eleven-team league. The Robins' record was won 15, drawn 1 and lost 4 in 20 matches, with 1,103 points for and 817 against. Mainstays of the team that season were Bob Roger, George White, Ian Williams, Ken Middleditch, Neil Street, Ernie Lessiter and Mike Broadbanks. Middleditch had come from Poole at the start of the season as part of the League's attempt to equalise the strength of the teams competing in the championship, and he formed a potent partnership with the top-scoring Bob Roger. Broadbanks came from Wembley on a £50 transfer fee, and though he performed only moderately in his first season he went on to become one of the Robins' all-time greats. Swindon won just one more championship, in the British League in 1967, but made a bright start to the new millennium with a Premier League Knock-out Cup win in 2000. The Premier League is one of two major leagues in British speedway, and fixtures take the Robins all over England and as far north as Scotland.

Still on a sporting theme, in April 1958 Swindon Town FC, on the brink of putting together a bright and creative young side that would be the talk of lower division football in the 1960s, bought the main grandstand from the Aldershot tattoo ground for a mere £3,400 at auction. Directors and officials made three inspection visits before deciding to bid for it. They considered it a splendid opportunity to provide the County Ground with a bigger and better stand at a bargain price, though the bill went up somewhat before the stand, originally 143 yards long and 30 feet wide, was re-erected along the Shrivenham Road side of the ground. There was also a smaller, two-tier stand on offer; Accrington Stanley bought that one for £1,450, though they scarcely had time to put it to use before money troubles put them out of business. Years later, the same could almost have been said about Swindon, one of the significant causes of their financial woes being a later grandstand which cost rather more than £3,400 to acquire.

Meanwhile, Councillor Mrs G.L. Knapp, brandishing a packet of first aid equipment which had cost her just 4s 5d, told Swindon Council that such a pack contained all that was necessary to equip a bus. She was protesting against the decision of the transport committee not to provide first aid kits on buses because any benefit would not justify the cost.

It was in 1958 that eleven-year-old Raymond O'Sullivan arrived in Swindon with his family from Waterford in Ireland. 'My Dad worked in the slaughterhouse of a meat factory in Waterford. My Mum ran a sweet shop. Home was a council house in the Cork

The best in the land: Swindon Robins' champion speedway team of 1957. (*C. Shailes*)

Road. The Swindon job came up because Dad's firm also had a factory there. Dad asked for the move because the money would be a lot better in Swindon,' the man who grew up to be the pop star Gilbert O'Sullivan later told an American interviewer. He went to St Joseph's Comprehensive in Swindon and then the art college where he played in various groups including the Doodles, the Prefects and Rick's Blues. He also spent hours pounding away at a piano that had been bought for his sister to play, until his mother thought it best to put it out in the shed. There he made his music, produced demo tapes and occasionally had things thrown at him by peace-loving neighbours. 'When I was at art school I formed a group, and I used to write songs and send the demos to people like Tony Hatch,' he recalled. 'They always sent them back unopened. I never got anywhere. When I'd finished college I told my mother I wanted to go to London to try my hand at music. I was good at art in the same way that I'd been good at history, but I never thought I was great. But I really thought that I could be, if I wasn't already, as good as anybody else at song writing.' He arrived in London in 1967 and lived a bedsit life as a sales clerk at C&A before his big break came; that was late in 1970 with his Christmas hit *Nothing Rhymed,* and six more Top Ten hits followed in the next three years, including two massive number ones in *Clair* and *Get Down.*

Like most bright young men going to London from the provinces, he did not have many kind words for the town he left behind; but then again, he only had to open his mouth to prove that he was Irish, so it was no wonder he later admitted to feeling a bit of a misfit and a loner, as well as 'the scruffy art student with painted jeans and long hair'. That said, he did not have too much that was negative to say about Swindon either, admitting that even within his family of two sisters and three brothers he was 'a bit of a black sheep'. His first great gimmicks were to appear in Bisto Kid clothes, call himself Gilbert on stage and sing apparently autobiographical songs about heartbreak, death and the need for approval; but in the end, he was not as different as all that from other young performers, apart from in his dazzling ability to write songs with beautiful and haunting melodies and arresting lyrics. Married with two daughters, he now lives in the Channel Islands and is always welcomed with open arms whenever he chooses to come back to the mainland to make music.

Gilbert O'Sullivan has continued to perform beyond his years of Top Ten stardom. (*BUP*)

In 1959 a social researcher named Pamela Brown interviewed a 5 per cent sample of families who had moved into council housing in Swindon from other parts of the country. A surprisingly large number of them, perhaps 80 per cent, appeared to have moved from substandard housing, so most were well satisfied with their new homes and gardens. Criticisms about council houses of the time generally were that the rooms were too small and the privacy inadequate, and Miss Brown ascribed people's wish to move away from them to a desire for more practical comfort and convenience rather than to any spirit of snobbery or 'keeping up with the Joneses'. Most of the families thought Swindon was an expensive place in which to live; on average, they paid 43s per week in rent, compared with 27s at their last address. Nevertheless, two-thirds of them thought it was worth it. In seven out of ten of the homes there was a family income of between £10 and £18 per week. There was outspoken criticism of their area's alleged lack of local amenities –

shops, parks, cinemas, theatres, schools and public transport – once the six-month 'honeymoon period' was over. The experts believed, however, that Swindon was being used as a scapegoat by people who had been uprooted from a familiar, settled environment to one in which change was constantly in the air. When it came to hard facts, fewer than 15 per cent of the 161 families Miss Brown interviewed said they wanted to leave Swindon, and she was left with the clear impression that in the end a number of these would eventually settle down. Meanwhile, she concluded, for those who were convinced that they ought to return to their roots, every minor upset was seen as further proof that Swindon was not the place for them.

The same year brought the end of the Empire Theatre on the corner of Victoria Road and Groundwell Road, though it had entertained its last patrons four years earlier. It had been the Queen's when it was built in 1898, but changed its name very shortly after Victoria's death in 1901. It was one of the few Swindon buildings that drew an admiring glance from John Betjeman, who admired its 'gay Flemish Renaissance' style. It could seat up to 1,600, and alternated between being a theatre and a cinema, which was its function between 1927 and 1949. The middle years of the century were no time to be trying to revive live theatre in great barns of Victorian buildings, and its demise after that was predictably swift. It was a pity, since the great Swindon film buff Brian Little reckoned that as a cinema the Empire 'had a very steep projection rake and a lovely atmosphere'.

The Swinging Sixties?

Princess Margaret Hospital in Okus Road was opened on Monday 4 January 1960, and it did not have to wait long for its first patient – 24-year-old Bernard Pecqueur of Silverton Road, Park North, an electro-plater with Plessey's in Kembrey Street, was brought in by car with acid burns to his arms and back after an accident at work. It was estimated that the hospital would cost some £2 million, though its expansion over the years, until late in the century, made a nonsense of that figure. Princess Margaret laid the foundation stone in April 1957, and returned to perform the official opening ceremony seven years later. PMH was a force for much good in the years it was open, from 1960 until late in 2002, when it was swept away to make way for housing, yet its story cannot be regarded as a happy one. Nobody in the early days would have dreamed that it would scarcely last long enough to see out the century, but there were early indications of trouble ahead, and problems which undermined Swindon's standing in the eyes of the rest of the country. According to the social historian Kenneth Hudson in 1967, soon after the hospital's Stage Two was completed: 'The windows left a lot to be desired. More precisely, daylight could be seen round the edges of the frames.' The problem was apparently in the men's orthopaedic department, where staff struggled to stem the draughts coming from half-inch gaps around the 20×8 feet windows. Those with an eye for symmetry were delighted that PMH's successor, at Commonhead, close to junction 15 of the M4, was planned to be named the Great Western Hospital, the cost of which has been conservatively estimated at £150 million. Back in 1960 the town's long-serving hospital of that name was closed the day after the designers Powell and Moya's shiny new creation opened up for the benefit of Mr Pecqueur – and countless others including the glamour girl Melinda Messenger, who was born there in February 1971.

In the early 1960s health was a burning issue, just as it is today. Forty years ago tuberculosis was not a complaint more often associated with cattle. In 1959 twenty-four people had died of pulmonary TB in Swindon, and in the spring of 1961 there was much publicity for an X-ray campaign in which, 'in the never-ending hunt for TB cases, the mass radiography unit is giving Swindon the most intensive cover ever. With as little trouble as it takes to vote, you can have your lungs photographed quite near your home.' The campaign was looking for 1,500 door-to-door canvassers, each of whom would have to visit no more than twenty houses over two weeks. 'If you would like to help in hunting and stamping out the unknown cases of TB in your area, now is your chance,' the organisers concluded; not that the town could ever have been seen as a hotbed of the disease. Those twenty-four deaths a year in Swindon might strike us as unacceptable today, but at the time they represented no more than half the national average.

The Beatles in the 1960s. Ringo had yet to join the group when it visited McIlroys in 1962.

But it wasn't all doom and gloom for Swindon's residents. Although it passed by all but the young and trendy at the time, the Beatles' performance at McIlroys Ballroom on 17 July 1962 has become one of those iconic moments in Swindon for the 'baby boomer' generation of postwar children. Ask anyone in town aged between fifty and sixty if they were at Mac's that night and they will say yes, of course they were, wouldn't have missed it for the world. It might reasonably be reckoned that there were at least ten thousand people in that hall above the store in Regent Street that night; it is surprising they did not all fall through the floor and end up in ladies' fashions. In fact, the true attendance figure was 360, hardly surprising since the Beatles were unknown much beyond Merseyside and Hamburg at that time. Their first hit, *Love Me Do*, was still three months away, and Ringo Starr was yet to replace Pete Best on drums. The only sign of the visit in the *Evening Advertiser* was the ballroom's standard advertisement, billing them as 'The Fabulous Beat Group from Liverpool' and 'The Most Popular Group in the North'; but then again, the band that came along the following week was doubtless given just as big a build-up. As Bill Reid, who promoted the show jointly with the colourful Dave Backhouse, recalled: 'People kept telling us they were going to have a hit record, but we heard this all the time.' Potential hit-makers or not, the Fab Four were paid just £27 10s for their gig at

McIlroys, but Bill knew they would be worth much, much more than that, and pulled off the coup of his life by advance booking them for Salisbury on 15 June 1963 – by which time they had been number one in the charts for five weeks with *From Me To You*. Their services cost £300 that time. Of the McIlroys visit, Bill said: 'They were a very unusual band. They just turned up in a van, got out and got up on stage. They were entirely different to the other bands around at the time, who were playing in gold lamé costumes.' It seems odd that this part of England staged some of the first Beatles concerts outside Liverpool or Germany. Bath and Stroud also saw them in their very early days, and the boys spent a happy little holiday at Weston-super-Mare at that time. Maybe Swindon was simply a convenient stopping-off place for Weston. Whatever, they provided a good night out for 360 youngsters – or should that be 10,000?

Even at the dawn of the 'swinging sixties' there was time to look back on a more traditional way of life in Swindon, and in 1962 the town's first public GWR museum opened in Faringdon Road. It was hailed as a major innovation, but the shortcomings of its restricted site became ever more apparent during the thirty-seven years it operated, and there were many changes, both in museum philosophy and presentation and in the growth from the mid-1960s of the railway preservation movement. This saw the development of an increasingly impressive GWR facility at the Didcot Railway Centre, as well as the hands-on and proactive Swindon & Cricklade Railway from the early 1980s. The quality of the exhibits on display at the museum was unquestionable, however, and they formed the bedrock of the modern Steam museum that has taken its place.

The big freeze of late 1962 and the early months of 1963 was legendarily severe, though not for very long in Swindon. There was what the local papers called 'Arctic' weather right into March, but evidence suggests it was not quite Arctic in a way a polar bear might understand the word; how much League football was played in a town was a good indication of just how much local life was disrupted, and Swindon Town did better than most in fulfilling their fixtures as arranged. The worst time was the immediate Christmas and New Year period, when 500 miles of roads in Wiltshire were blocked and there were long delays in reopening the routes from Swindon to Highworth, Malmesbury, Devizes and Marlborough. Garrard's reported that a quarter of their workers had failed to get in; at Pressed Steel, some 500 were absent, and the difficulty of bringing supplies in and sending goods out resulted in 700 men being sent home; at high-tech Vickers Armstrong in South Marston one worker from Highworth helped keep the wheels of industry turning by coming to work on her horse. Shivering council tenants at Barton Road complained that their back boilers were simply unequal to the task; Swindon's much-loved Golden Lion statue crumbled away; and food shortages put up the price of both carrots and cabbage by 2d per pound, to 10d and 1s respectively. Of course there were groans about profiteering, but this was one time when most people really did accept that the farmers and wholesalers were struggling.

THE HUMMELFLUG SUMMER

The Beatles' appearance at McIlroys Ballroom in 1962 was proof that Swindon's beat music scene was more vibrant than anything that could be boasted by most other towns of a similar size, and so it went on through the 1960s. Those who can remember those times look back with particular affection on the summer of 1964, where there was music not only at McIlroys and the Locarno but at any number of smaller venues, from Club X to the Ship, Walcot Boys' Club in Buckhurst Crescent, Shrivenham Memorial Hall . . . Within just a few weeks in May, June and July McIlroys or the Locarno hosted the Hollies, Dave Berry and the Cruisers, the Animals, the Mojos, the Applejacks, the Rockin' Berries, Millie, Peter and Gordon, Tony Orlando and Sounds Incorporated. Even the folk club at the Whitehouse in Station Road showcased Julie Felix, nearly six years before she had her big British hit with *El Condor Pasa*. There was also a bewildering number of Wiltshire bands playing in Swindon and its surroundings, leaving aside Dave Dee, Dozy, Beaky, Mick and Tich, the eight-times Top Ten entrants from Salisbury. Groups recalled with varying degrees of affection include the Strangers and the Whispers, who were regulars at McIlroys, plus the Trutones, the Hummelflugs, the Strychneens, the Burnettes, Terry and the Freelancers, Tony and the Tempos, Ricky Vernon and the Pathfinders, the Fonetiks, the Senators, the Zephyrs, Linda Lane and the Sinners, the Saints, the Alpines, Vern Rogers and the Orbits. But not everything was wild and way-out. Throughout the beat heyday, there was still work at McIlroys for the likes of Harry Smith and his Orchestra and Ken Exton with his trumpet and band. And the streets of the town resounded to a far more traditional beat on 8 May, when hundreds of men and women took part in a procession to mark the granting of the Freedom of the Borough to the air base at RAF Lyneham.

Not everybody was impressed by Swindon's cultural facilities. The town's MP, Francis Noel-Baker, told the Swindon Artists' Society's annual general meeting that local cultural facilities were 'lagging behind the size of the population', and told of far smaller communities that did better when it came to staging and enjoying the arts.

In 1965 the Wiltshire Education Committee announced that schooling in the county would cost £12.5 million in 1965. This represented a rise of £7.73 million in seven years. The expansion of Swindon was a major factor in this, as was the growing number of armed forces families. In 1957–8 the gross expenditure on education in Wiltshire was just £4,725,000. Eight years later teachers' salaries alone accounted for that amount, and the Education Committee was told that schooling now represented more than 60 per cent of county revenue expenditure and 75 per cent of capital expenditure.

In May 1966 the *Evening Advertiser* estimated that, while more people from Swindon were going abroad on holiday, probably only about a quarter of the population went away at all, and of these only a quarter or less went abroad. The paper reported the AV Travel Agency as saying that Spain, Portugal and Italy were the most popular overseas destinations, and holidays by express coaches to a single beach resort were the most widely sought, rather than coach touring: 'This is probably because it is not only one of the cheapest ways of getting a holiday abroad, but because many who take this kind of holiday do so for one reason only – to be really sure of some sun.' There was also an increase in people asking for air package holidays by charter flight, again largely for single resorts. Switzerland and Austria were both popular, and Express Coaches expected their Austrian resorts to be in brisk demand with Swindon holidaymakers. Interest in Yugoslavia, Romania, Bulgaria and Tunisia was increasing. Greece and the Greek Islands

The scene in Regent Street in the 1960s. Few would deny that Swindon was in need of a new lease of life.

were not as popular as these destinations, but things seemed to be on the move. 'Quite a few people from Swindon have decided on Greece this year,' said the manager of one agency. At much the same time, the social historian Kenneth Hudson interviewed the manager of what he described as Swindon's principal travel agent, and this professional made three general comments. First, his branch was less profitable than any other in his group, since the average booking in Swindon tended to be about £20 smaller than elsewhere, while involving just as much work; secondly, that a high proportion of his customers were married couples in their fifties and sixties, living in the humbler streets of old Swindon; and thirdly that, here in the middle years of the 1960s, he had never to his recollection booked a winter sports holiday from the Swindon branch.

In 1967 Kenneth Hudson published *An Awkward Size For a Town*, subtitled 'A study of Swindon at the 100,000 mark'. In it, he wrote of 'the image of a quaintly old-fashioned, comic-opera town that tries hard but has never really succeeded in pulling itself into the modern age. The image is fortunately getting a little frayed, but it persists, despite the great changes which have transformed Swindon during the past 20 years, and it represents a real obstacle to attracting the variety of people and the range of development which are so badly needed . . .' Mr Hudson caused some outrage when, remarking that 'only the most sterling characters can remain completely unmoved when holiday acquaintances smile at the mention of Swindon', he suggested the borough might

The aptly named *Evening Star*, built in 1960, was the last steam locomotive to be built at Swindon. *(Tim King)*

consider a change of name. Later experience of the hated name change to Thamesdown, which lasted only twenty-three years after 1974, would have told him just what a sticking point that is. Mr Hudson also told a meeting of his wish to see the railway station modernised and a move away from over-emphasis on the railway industry, and both these ideas sparked 'an interesting series of explosions'. One objector said the name Swindon might not derive at all from 'pig town', but from the Anglo-Saxon for 'the crooked path up the hill'. Another argued that if the GWR really had been paternalistic, then it had been a very good father. It was clear that even in the dying days of the Railway Works, its influence would not easily be forgotten.

Certainly the 125th anniversary of the GWR Works came at a strange time in Swindon's history, in a town anxious to catch up with a 1960s building boom that had all but passed it by in that decade. In 1969, the year when man first walked on the moon, much of the Victorian structure of the New Town was still in place. Yet change was afoot,

and while a shiny new shopping centre would be part of that revolution, the increasingly doubtful future of the Works occupied just as many people's minds in that anniversary year. Nevertheless, that did not stop people from looking back with pride to 1843, and the events leading up to the future Sir Daniel Gooch being instructed by the GWR to recommend a site for a locomotive maintenance depot between London and Bristol:

> On full consideration I reported in favour of Swindon, it being the junction with the Cheltenham branch and also a convenient division of the GW line for the engine working. Mr Brunel and I went to look at the ground, then only green fields, and he agreed with me as to its being the best place.

That decision transformed Swindon from a hilltop village with a population of 2,000 in 1841 to a town of 100,000 by 1968.

Some of Swindon Town's 1969 Wembley heroes more than thirty years on, with manager Danny Williams and goalscoring star Don Rogers holding the League Cup. Second from the left on the back row is one of their Arsenal foes that afternoon, the Scottish international Frank McLintock. (*BUP*)

There aren't many fairy tales in this book; Swindon does not tend to lend itself to stories of high-flown fantasy. In 1969, though, the town amazed the world, or at least that part of the world that sets great store by the winning of football matches at Wembley. Swindon Town, from the third highest division in the country, beat top-flight Arsenal 3–1 in the final of the League Cup – and after extra time, too, when tradition has it that the highly trained major teams usually win through. A few provisos need to be added – if only to be instantly dismissed. The first is that this was only the ninth League Cup final, and the big clubs had been notoriously slow to take the competition seriously; then again, the mighty Leeds United were the winners in the previous year, and in the following season the cup went to the Manchester City team graced by Bell, Lee and the old County Ground favourite Mike Summerbee. Arsenal were sleeping giants, having won nothing since the early 1950s; then again, they would soon confound everyone by winning the League and FA Cup double in 1971, and several members of that team had turned out against Swindon at Wembley. Finally, it must be said that Swindon would not be a Third Division side for much longer, securing promotion a few weeks after the final; nevertheless, they still started the match as distant second favourites, and this time it was the classic 'Soccer's Mr Football' sports reporter Desmond Hackett who was called upon to eat his pre-match words – and his hat. The team was not the brilliant young home-grown side of a few years before, but it still had John Trollope and more importantly it still had Don Rogers – not to mention Rod Thomas, Stan Harland, Roger Smart, Peter Noble . . . Swindon scored first after 35 minutes, when Smart capitalised on a terrible mix-up involving Arsenal's goalie Bob Wilson. With 6 minutes left there was a goalkeeping disaster at the other end and Arsenal were level through Bobby Gould, but Swindon heads did not drop and in appalling conditions – the once-hallowed Wembley turf was a disgrace thirty years ago – Rogers seized extra time by the scruff of the neck and hammered home goals two and three. Many men in Swindon feel they should be able to remember the celebrations in town that night – but for some reason it's all a bit hazy . . .

Swindon Transformed

On 17 December 1970 work began on the Brunel Centre, the redevelopment at the heart of Swindon's shopping and commercial centre. Until long after the Second World War Regent Street had dominated the local shopping scene, and the council recognised that with the railway industry in serious decline radical changes would be necessary to make the town attractive to new enterprises and, not least, to the people who would staff them. The Parade was the first step in this direction, but this paled into insignificance as the 1960s progressed and planners dreamed of far grander schemes. The Brunel Centre was the result, and it was a project that succeeded on many more points than it failed. For a start, shoppers and experts alike liked the look of the first phase, the big Plaza building, which was surrounded by a transparent canopy and a stainless steel fascia which not only kept out the rain but hinted subtly at Victorian railway architecture. Secondly, great care was taken not to disrupt existing trade more than was absolutely necessary, to the extent that the final piece of this first jigsaw, the Regent Street flank, was not put into place until 1975. A pleasing touch was the incorporation of the façade of the inter-war Marks & Spencer building into the new block, in acknowledgement of the fact that people do not wish to lose their bearings completely in their home town. This spirit came to the fore again when it came to allocating space in the building. They say the Centre can be compared with the Galleria in Milan – but the approach to shopping provision was strictly feet-on-the-ground, with Sainsbury's being the first store opened.

The completion of the Brunel Centre took up most of the 1970s, by the end of which Swindon had an extra 50,000 square metres of shopping space, as well as new offices, flats and public spaces. The David Murray John Building, twenty storeys high and offering a good deal of living accommodation as well as offices, gave the town a new focal point which again combined striking modernism with echoes of industrial architecture. Perhaps what strikes the visitor most, however, is how this monumental building fits happily into a commercial area that is strictly on the human scale, a shopping area that is big and bright but reassuringly manageable. Even today, the little Victorian streets lap up against the Brunel Centre in parts, reminding us of the humble terraces that made way for it, and of the unassuming place Swindon was before it came. All that has changed – but in its twenty-first-century way the town centre still has a relaxed and easy-going face.

There is a well-known photograph of the queen opening the first stage of Swindon Civic Centre from the pavilion in Theatre Square on 5 November 1971. She is surrounded by men who symbolise establishment order in the regions – the Lord Lieutenant, the church, the military, the police, the mayor – and even the pouring rain speaks of unchanging times, since it rained on her coronation and managed to do so on most of

Some distinguished modern buildings have sprung up in Swindon over the past few decades, but none is more of a landmark for the town than the central David Murray John Building.

Theatre Square in the early 2000s. The Wyvern Theatre is still professional and inviting, but the pavilion from which the queen once addressed the townsfolk is looking decidedly down at heel.

SWINDON CIVIC CENTRE
INAUGURATED BY THE QUEEN
5 NOVEMBER 1971

her big days after that, at least until the triumph of the 2002 Golden Jubilee celebrations. It is a scene of hope and high expectation – but the somewhat sorry state of the pavilion today is a reminder of the constant need for vigilance, care for the environment and yes, of course, the money to keep facilities up to scratch. Unfortunately, this quite important corner of town must be placed decidedly into the file labelled 'Could Do Better'.

In 1972, the year in which the first phase of the Brunel Centre was opened, Swindon's railway station was also given a major facelift. It was a move that had to be made, but it was painful for all that, since the original had played such a significant rôle in the town's history. If you think today's station is functional and unimpressive, you can be assured that the old one was no better. The Great Western was prepared to lavish fortunes on its termini if it so wished, as Paddington and Bristol Temple Meads remind us to this day, but the town that housed its great works was treated to an architectural essay on the mundane. Back in the mid-1960s the social commentator Kenneth Hudson saw a more prepossessing railway station as essential to Swindon regaining its self-confidence and pride, but he was shot down in flames from almost every quarter. All that changed in 1972, as life was changing all over town at that time; another big development was the arrival of Burmah Oil in Marlborough Road. Britain in general looks back on the 1960s as the great time of kicking over the architectural traces, but the revolution was a little late in rolling into Swindon.

Isambard Kingdom Brunel, who gave life to industrial Swindon and lent his name to its shopping centre well over a century later, was often photographed against awesome symbols of the mechanical age. It was thus fitting that when a statue was put up in his honour close to the Brunel Centre, it was high above Havelock Square atop and surrounded by riveted gunmetal grey cylinders. It was an imaginative piece of symbolism that pleased even those who were offended by the fact that he was placed with his back to the Railway Works and the main line, though central Swindon can be so confusing to all but the most finely attuned orienteers that

The brooding presence of I.K. Brunel looks across Havelock Square – and away from the railway.

Old Town memories in High Street and Wood Street.

it seems not the most heinous of gaffes. The statue was unveiled on 29 March 1973 by Sir James Jones, Permanent Secretary at the Department of the Environment.

On 1 April 1974 came the century's biggest shake-up of local government organisation, with in some cases whole counties swept away for reasons that were not always altogether clear. There were howls of protest as residents of shires dating back into the mists of time suddenly found themselves in such alien territory as Avon, Cleveland or Merseyside; some towns, too, suffered a similar fate, and so it was that Thamesdown was born out of Swindon Borough and Highworth Rural District Councils. A few years earlier the social historian Kenneth Hudson had detected a deep distrust of any name change, but in 1974 opposition to the concept was not overwhelming. As the chairman of the new authority's policy and resources committee, Councillor A.J. Masters, commented:

> Thamesdown inherits a lively and vigorous local authority. In considering future policies, the new council intends to pursue a programme of substantial housing development, further industrial diversification and leisure provision . . . The council intends to initiate a new corporate plan with particular bias towards environmental improvement and housing.

Come 1997, after a chequered history of both triumphs and tribulations, disaffection with the authority was such that the decision to readopt the name Swindon was made with scarcely a backward glance when the authority was granted the unitary status Thamesdown had always craved. This gave it power over local education and social services, and life in both spheres has proved almost frighteningly tough since then. What is certain is that power, under any name, can be an awesome burden.

ROMAN SWINDON?

Just before Christmas 1975 Roman remains thought to date back to AD 200 were discovered on a site in Old Town. Pieces of pottery – cooking pots and tableware – were found in an archaeological 'rescue' dig near the Square. Since the experts had only two months to salvage what they could before developers moved in, they were anxious for more volunteers to help in what promised to be an interesting few weeks. They had also unearthed what they believed could have been part of a paved area outside a Roman building, as well as medieval remains. 'What we have found is the first evidence of Roman settlement on this side of Swindon,' said the field director, Bernard Phillips.

THE OASIS – A MIRAGE?

The Oasis leisure centre opened in January 1976, proof positive that going swimming could be fun for children. It reminded some lucky people of the great resort complexes they had visited on holiday, with its wave machine, choice of three mighty tube slides which snaked out of the futuristic dome before depositing you in a plunge pool at the bottom, and a shipwreck for the little ones to play on. Most visitors, though, had simply never seen anything like it in their lives, and it became *the* place for birthday party outings for families in a wide area of Wiltshire and Gloucestershire, to the extent that two million people had used it by the end of its third year. It also taught many people the somewhat painful lesson that Swindon was expanding rapidly to the west, and was not shaping up to be an easy town to get around. More than a quarter of a century on the Oasis has expanded to take in other sports, indoor and out; and essentially it continues to deliver the goods for all who like it as it is, though as with most other public places of its age a few tens of thousands of pounds spent in sprucing it up would not go amiss. What it is not is an Olympic-sized pool, which is what some keen swimmers hoped it would be. In fact in the mid-1970s 'an Olympic-sized pool' was on the shopping list of most towns, rather as skateboard parks were in the early 2000s. Few were built, and understandably so, since they are huge and of value to only a small minority. Far better used has been the pool's adjoining sports hall, not least for shows and concerts. They even say the Gallagher brothers from Manchester named their band Oasis after a successful gig here, but most outsiders see the story as some monstrous Swindon urban myth, on a par with the one about the granny rolled up in a blanket on the roof rack of the stolen car . . .

LOST LANDMARKS

Today's version of the Golden Lion dates from 1977, and it must be said it is looking its age. The original Golden Lion was to be found not far away from where its successor now reclines, in the forecourt of the pub of the same name that stood beside the Wilts & Berks

Pre-millennium dome. The Oasis may not be the state-of-the-art facility it once was, but it still gives a lot of people in Swindon a lot of fun.

Canal off Bridge Street. It was a well-loved old thing; little children would climb all over it, and laddish young men would swear that it roared if a virgin walked by. It was moved when the pub was demolished in 1956, and came to a sad end when, in supposed safe-keeping in the corporation yard, it became damp under its wraps and cracked in the frost in the hard winter of 1962/3. The plan had always been to resite it; instead, to mark the queen's Silver Jubilee, a new lion was commissioned by the council from Carleton Attwood, who has made his mark on the town with various other sculptures, including the splendid Harold Fleming at the County Ground. Mr Attwood's work, with a time capsule in its plinth, was removed in the mid-1990s for redevelopment work at the Brunel Centre, but is now back in Canal Walk, facing resolutely towards Regent Street.

The loss in 1978 of the large and impressive Baptist Tabernacle at the top of Regent Street was mourned by people far beyond its dwindled congregation. It was built in 1886 at a cost of £5,798, and its six mighty columns and portico made it one of the half-dozen most imposing buildings in town. Its end came after five of the town's free churches – the Baptists, the Methodists, Trinity and Sandford Street United Reformed Churches and Broad Street Church of Christ – had banded together to form Swindon Central Churches Council. This clearly called for a rationalisation of buildings and the huge Tabernacle, originally built with seating for a thousand, was a prime candidate for closure in hard financial times; parts of it had already become unusable, and it was argued that repairs would not be a good investment. The last service there took place on 3 July 1977, when three former ministers helped lead the worship. Demolition came in the following year. The joint churches did not have a finer site in town, so it was there that they built their new red-brick Central Church Pilgrim Centre, complete with an inexpensive café which helps keep the place buzzing almost every day. It even has a mini-portico, but it can hardly be said that it echoes the original weighty structure. As for those six mighty columns, they were bought by a Malmesbury man who planned to incorporate them into a country house; *Dallas* was a popular television show at

The Golden Lion, mark II. Created to commemorate the Silver Jubilee of 1977, it is already looking its age and more.

A reminder of just how much the Baptist Tabernacle was part of the Regent Circus scene. What an astonishing house front the pillars would have created if the planners had allowed the man who bought them to have his way.

the time and the planners, fearing that a not-so-mini Southfork Ranch was about to descend on the Wiltshire countryside, refused him permission to build. For years the columns stood in sections in a builder's yard, gradually disappearing beneath weeds and undergrowth – a sad end for one of the Nonconformists' most notable contributions to the Swindon townscape of old.

SCIENCE IS FUN

In 1979 the Science Museum took over the redundant Wroughton airfield, a Second World War base which was opened in 1940 to modify and prepare aircraft for front-line stations – and was so good at its job that sixty-two different types of aircraft were handled there. The

The Pilgrim Centre took the place of the Tabernacle. Its small portico is a nod towards what was here before.

museum took on the site first and foremost as a storage facility for the bigger objects in its collection, ranging from an enormous Lockheed Constellation airliner and prototype computers, to a wood press weighing 140 tonnes and early MRI scanners. Other extremely rare aircraft include the oldest surviving British airliner, the De Havilland Dragon Orcadian, and the all-metal monoplane Boeing 247. Seven hangars are used in all, and the air and other popular collections are stored for easy viewing. The museum is not open daily, and it is best to telephone for informatiom. Groups of fifteen or more can also book guided tours. The best way to see the museum, however, is on one of its big weekend open days, when you can view its exhibits alongside other visiting attractions. Several of these are held during the year, but the most popular by far tend to be the Wiltshire Steam and Vintage Gathering, a classic country fair in early June; a Drive weekend at the end of that month, when there is the chance to sit behind the wheel of buses, lorries, fork-lift trucks and JCBs; the wonderful Wroughton Nostalgia Show in late July, one of the biggest vintage vehicle shows in the UK; and the Heritage Open Days in September, when the spotlight turns on the museum site itself, its architectural heritage and the part it played in the Second World War.

THE SHOPPING SPREE

Despite all the concrete and glass, Swindon and its people still needed some convincing that here was a shopping centre to compete with the best. Enter the chamber of commerce, with a Shopping Spree festival of fun that would confound the cynics who said: 'Nobody would come here from out of town for a shopping day out.' The first Spree was in 1978, and was such a success that they planned an even more ambitious programme for 1979. What did not change was the choice of Mickey Mouse, Donald Duck and other Disney characters to mix and mingle and help bring in the crowds. A new age of marketing was dawning.

Perhaps it all proved too great an attraction for some youngsters. A Swindon mother of five told magistrates that she was prepared to go to prison in protest against her children being forced to stay on at school until they were sixteen. She refused to pay a £25 fine imposed on her because of their non-appearance at class, and asked: 'What are you supposed to do? Carry them in?'

The End of the Century

As a sign of more adventurous times in Swindon, in 1980 Wendy Buonaventura was offering a day-course in belly dancing at the Thamesdown Community Arts Studio – a chance to 'indulge your mind and body in an unusual, sensuous and traditional art form' and one that was open to 'anyone – whatever shape, size or age'. This being the dawning of the age of equal opportunities, the advertisement implied an open-ended invitation to men to go along, but as it turned out – and to the relief of all concerned – none did.

In a rather more traditional educational setting, the schools of today encourage their students to be part of a caring society and play an active part in community life, but this is only a fairly recent phenomenon. For long enough they were simply places of learning, plus any out-of-hours activities the staff saw fit to promote. In 1981 sixth-formers at Headlands School pointed the way ahead when they raised enough money to buy expensive kitchen equipment and two sewing machines for the Hawthorn Centre for handicapped people in Cricklade Road. Non-uniform days, raffles and lunchtime discos raised £210, and Hambro Life then contributed another £200 to the fund which provided electric and manual sewing machines and equipment including a toaster, scales, a food mixer and liquidiser and a slow cooker. Several students had built up a close relationship with the Centre over the years, often popping in to chat with its users and lend a hand. The school also supported children's charities such as the NSPCC and Dr Barnardo's, and hoped to collect £900 towards the maintenance of its minibus through an 11-mile sponsored walk from Avebury to Coate Water.

In a similarly charitable manner, in the early 1980s enthusiasts banded together to form the Swindon & Cricklade Railway, which is Wiltshire's only standard gauge heritage railway and one for which there are exciting plans in the years ahead. It must be said they have done, and are still doing, well. All they really had to work on was the site of Blunsdon station and part of the track bed of what was originally the Midland & South Western Junction Railway. After that they simply used their knowledge, imagination and any funds available to acquire the rolling stock, track, locomotives and buildings that can be seen today, and what they have created adds up to an interesting place to be on a fine weekend afternoon, complete with a café. The track runs for half a mile or so to a station, signal-box and engine shed at Hayes Knoll, which again are modern creations. Steam rides can be enjoyed on this stretch of line on special days, and diesel rides on other Sunday afternoons, but planning approval has been given for a mile of new track from the Blunsdon to Moulden Hill country park on the edge of North Swindon. Eventually the society hopes to develop this into a circular route, with a station at the Sparcells housing

The Swindon & Cricklade Railway's station and centre at Blunsdon. GWR locomotive no. 3845, built in Swindon in 1942, is one of the enthusiasts' restoration projects.

estate, but that lies in the future. So do eventual plans to extend the line in the opposite direction, towards Cricklade. The Midland & South Western Junction Railway ran for just under 60 route miles between Andover and Andoversford, a small Cotswold community near Cheltenham. It was formed in 1891 but had a disastrous trading history before being grouped with the Great Western Railway in 1923. Blunsdon, the last station to open in 1895, was little more than a halt for milk trains, and in 1924 it was one of the first to close to passenger services. Goods traffic ceased stopping there in 1937, but the line somehow struggled on under British Railways until 1961. Now new life is stirring at Blunsdon, and it is heartening to see that memories of railway life extend beyond Swindon's GWR heritage.

Swindon's success as a shopping centre ushered in its first park-and-ride scheme, as a temporary measure only, in the weeks leading up to Christmas 1983. The pressure on town centre parking over the Christmas period the previous year had led to scenes of chaos at the busiest times, with traders fearing that the shopping streets would end up the victims of their own popularity. The council was determined that there should be no repeat performance, and by August its technical services director John Daws was weighing up the pros and cons of two routes:

> So far specific sites have not been found, but the scheme could operate from car parks in Mannington and Greenbridge. A possible route for the Mannington end could be via Wootton Bassett and Kingshill Roads, with a stop at Commercial Road. The Greenbridge route would go along Stratton and Shrivenham roads to end at the Fleming Way/Debenhams lay-by. Regular bus services at least every 10 or 15 minutes and a short travel time would be vital if the scheme was to be successful.

At the time, the cost of short-term parking for up to two hours in town was set to go up from 30p to 40p – a move that would raise an extra £60,000 a year.

THE WRITING ON THE WALL

Artist Ken White, creator of many of the murals for which Swindon had become well known by this time, spent a week in late summer restoring one of his earliest creations, a scene of the Golden Lion Bridge. Thamesdown Community Arts threw itself wholeheartedly into commissioning murals in the 1970s, with varying results. Some have survived and look good; some are still there but are a little tired; some have been vandalised out of existence; and some, like the astonishing George and Dragon in Manton Street, were created on buildings which are simply not there any more. Arguably the first mural in Swindon was on the side of Hinder's pet shop on the corner of Commercial Road and Temple Street in the 1950s. The work of the signwriter Charles Gaze, it was on one level no more than an advertisement for the firm's bird-seed, 'Packed amid the pure air of the Wiltshire Downs', but its huge rustic script was so off-beat and arresting, filling the gable end, that people used to go on little detours to see it while they were in town, and thus the concept of murals for fun took hold.

The 1980s were famously a time when property developers and others with a keen eye for business grew rich. To their credit, they could also be imaginative and lavish in their

One of the most striking of the early murals with which Swindon has adorned itself in recent years. The medium seems to lend itself particularly well to pictures with industrial themes.

A reminder that not all the town's street art is two-dimensional – or heavy industrial.

The only way to photograph the windmill at Windmill Hill Business Park – reflected in the windows of one of its near neighbours.

spending of their wealth, and that certainly applied to the St Martin's Property Group when they introduced a splendid windmill into the futuristic glass and concrete environment of their Windmill Hill Business Centre in West Swindon. In a project that began in October 1983 and was completed in August 1984, they transferred the remains of the brick tower of the Chiseldon mill to the new site, and topped it with a canopy and sails copied as accurately as possible from a photograph taken in Chiseldon in 1881 by a local clergyman. The mill was originally built in 1823 and was still grinding corn until 1894, after which its tower was converted into a water storage tank. The West Swindon site had been known as Windmill Hill for centuries, after a mill that had stood there since medieval times. The developers' determination to commemorate the fact, and the expense they went to in order to do so, are much to be admired; sadly, such gestures are few and far between these days.

SEEING THE SEE

In October 1985 the new Church of England Bishop of Bristol, the Right Revd Barry Rogerson, hit upon the idea of running a special train – an InterCity Episcopuffer – to take members of his flock to his enthronement at Bristol Cathedral. His diocese stretches along the M4 corridor, with Swindon at one end and Bristol at the other, but the advantage of travelling by train was that it took in Chippenham, the see's third largest population centre. The 40-mile journey started from Swindon's parcel platform, where the bishop and his wife Olga were greeted by the Deputy Lord Lieutenant of Wiltshire, Field Marshal Sir Roland Gibbs. Members of Swindon's twenty-six Anglican parish congregations flocked to wish the new bishop well, and after Cricklade Deanery had presented him with a crozier, the traditional bishop's crook, he blessed the people of Thamesdown. He had a special thought for those with uncertain futures. 'I have had lots of letters and have been following carefully the proposed closure of the railway works,' he said. 'I have been involved in other places where these things happened, and people's

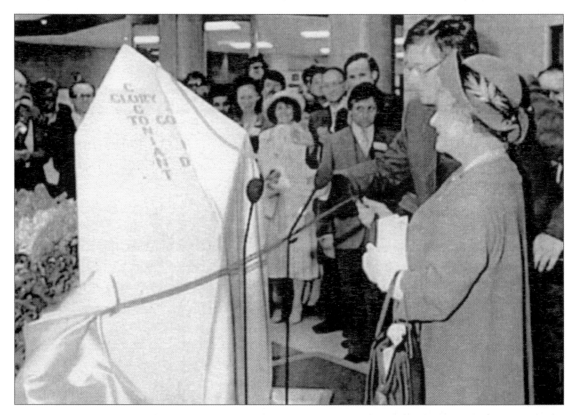

The Queen Mother, patron of the Bible Society for fifty-nine years, unveils a plaque to commemorate her opening of the organisation's new headquarters at the Delta Business Park in Westlea in May 1986. (*BUP*)

anxieties are close to me.' At just after 11am the train pulled out of Swindon in bright sunshine, *en route* for a similar stop at Chippenham, and from there on to Bristol for the enthronement. Bishop Barry, who retires in November 2002, was always keen for Swindon to know that, while it was as far away as it could be from Bristol, the town meant as much to him as anywhere else in the diocese; the presence today of a Bishop of Swindon is ample proof of that.

END OF THE LINE

The final closure of the GWR Works in 1986 was not the shock it would have been even thirty years before. Indeed, closure in, say, 1956 would not have been just a shock – it would have been unthinkable. It simply could not have happened. Swindon by then had ceased to be a one-industry town, as it all but was at the turn of the twentieth century, but to contemplate the closure of the Works would have been as absurd as it was sacrilegious. By the time it happened there had been warnings enough, lay-offs enough, snubs and setbacks and disappointments enough. In the 1980s, if you were in a lame duck industry, you were left in no doubt about it. The prime minister of the day's view of the future of the railways was such that on the occasions when she actually travelled by train, the novelty of the situation was such that it was commented upon in the newspapers. Not that the decline of rail can be put down to any individual's opinions, for it had been a long, miserable road. After nationalisation in 1948 locomotives built to GWR designs continued to be produced for a while, but there was a gradual decline in the fortunes of the Works, as of course there was in steam locos all over the western world, and in 1960 came the last of the line at Swindon, the appropriately named *Evening Star*. In 1963 a large part of the carriage works was closed, and activity was concentrated on the area west of the Cheltenham line – a stark contrast with the situation in 1935, when the site covered 326 acres. The end of diesel locomotive production was the last straw, and British Rail Engineering Ltd closed the works after 143 years of operation. It says much about the progress made in developing other employment opportunities that Swindon could withstand the blow; but, with a deep sadness shared by so many then, and by an ageing minority of residents today, withstand it it did.

JUDGING JEFFERIES

The year 1987 brought the centenary of the death of Richard Jefferies, the writer whose cottage beside the Sun Inn on Marlborough Road, Coate, is open as a museum on every first and third Sunday afternoon in summer. His family had farmed there since 1800, but the house was sold in 1877 when Jefferies left Swindon to pursue his writing career in London. Then aged just twenty-eight, he had only ten more years to live. He is best remembered for his country writing and treatises on farming and for two troubled late works, *The Story of My Heart*, which discusses his unorthodox beliefs, and *After London*, which depicts the city under a foetid swamp. The old farmhouse was bought by Swindon Corporation in 1926 at the instigation of Reuben George, the former mayor and inveterate backer of liberal and educational causes; and the first museum was opened there in 1960, since when it has been expanded to reflect, in particular, the writer's

Literary shrine: Richard Jefferies' birthplace.

interest in country life. This is an author who is not without honour in his own country, for the Richard Jefferies Society is committed to keeping his flame alive.

EXPANSION

In September 1988, in the wake of a three-week public enquiry held in Swindon late in 1987, the Environment Secretary Nicholas Ridley gave permission for ten thousand new homes – 'a town the size of Salisbury' – to be built on 1,500 acres between Haydon Wick and Penhill in the south and Blunsdon and St Andrew in the North. Both Wiltshire and Thamesdown Councils had originally opposed the plan, but they withdrew their opposition. Wiltshire accepted a £30 million offer from the development consortium, including £18 million towards improving roads in the area and sites for seven primary schools, a secondary school, a library and social services facilities. Thamesdown at first attacked the deal as a sell-out, but later accepted a package worth nearly £10 million for four community centres, two churches, major sports facilities and £2.7 million to be used for community and social purposes. Another major objector to withdraw its opposition was Swindon Health Authority after the consortium said it planned to build three health centres and houses for handicapped, mentally ill and elderly people. Despite all this, Thamesdown's planning chairman, Councillor Derrick Bye, was far from happy. 'This is a very sad day for Swindon,' he said. 'The effects will be enormous on the off-site infrastructure, the town centre, Princess Margaret Hospital . . . There will be a lot of pressure on them all . . . It will change the nature of the town and overstretch everything there is; the roads and services will not be able to cope. We really are going to suffer over the next ten years.'

A long way from the Railway Works: Civic cars roll along the Honda production line at South Marston. (*BUP*)

A year later, in 1989, Honda announced its decision to locate its UK manufacturing operations in Swindon. It was perhaps not the most obvious choice for a company with a history of antagonism towards trade unions, since Rover had been in the area for years with its highly unionised body-parts stamping plant. Many local politicians were taken by surprise by the move to South Marston, but Honda liked the ex-airfield site and appreciated Swindon's excellent communications. According to the industrial analyst Andrew Mair, the company was looking for very specific requirements from its Swindon workers:

> Nobody is recruited against a job description; all necessary training takes place in-house, so Honda has complete control over it. Recruits are not viewed as 'moronic clay' to be moulded to Honda's requirements, but as people who have achieved and will be able to achieve. They should therefore be strong individuals, but Honda avoids those with pre-formed mindsets. Open minds, flexibility, commitment – these are the key. Who would be the ideal recruit? 'A farmer would be ideal,' according to the engine plant manager. 'He is probably used to having to rely on his own initiative when he repairs his tractor.'

Farmers or not, there were 2,000 workers or 'associates' at Honda by 1994, and with the latest Civic models now rolling off the production lines of a vastly expanded plant at South Marston, that figure today is 4,000. The move has even meant that thousands of Swindon-built Hondas are being sent to Japan every year. The new £130 million factory, opened alongside the original in September 2001, has given Swindon the ability to produce 250,000 vehicles a year, with plans to export some 120,000 of these. Talk of

A long way from Beijing: set amid modern housing, though with the Peatmoor Lagoon close by, the Chinese Experience is an experience indeed, both inside and out.

success stories can so often backfire, but it is very hard to see Honda's history at South Marston as anything but.

The year 1989 also brought a quite astonishing addition to the landscape of West Swindon: the mighty pagoda of the Chinese Experience restaurant, set in more than 2.5 acres of grounds beside the Peatmoor Lagoon. Coming at the end of a decade that had seen so much of old Swindon die as the high tech years dawned, this strange new shape encouraged those who embraced change to feel that times really were a-changing – while convincing the die-hards that they had seen everything, now, in the town's rush to kick over the traces. Nobody ever grumbled about the food, however, or the appeal of the authentic Chinese furnishings, and a programme of live entertainment has made it a big draw for the disco and karaoke crowd on selected nights. Chinese New Year is one of the annual highlights, with traditional entertainment ranging from Chinese acrobats to dragon dancing and oriental musicians. Any number of towns and cities might claim they do this or that better than Swindon does, but it is unlikely that many of them can come up with any building quite as enjoyably outrageous as the Chinese Experience.

. . . AND RELEGATION

Of all the heartaches involved in being a Swindon Town supporter, nothing else remotely plumbed the depths experienced on 7 June 1990 when the Football League snatched away the First Division place won by the club in the end-of-season play-offs, and relegated them to the Third Division instead for thirty-six breaches of League rules, all but one of them involving irregular payments to players. What made matters worse was that the First Division was then what the Premiership is now – the very top of the pile – and Town had never previously been anywhere near it. There was great anguish in Swindon, with countless people who had never previously shown the slightest interest in the game joining in marches and rallies. The feeling, above all, was of a small club being bullied – and whatever the sin, it did not warrant losing two levels of seniority. Maybe all the marching worked; in any event, the League changed its decision to allow Town to stay put in the Second – from which, two years later, they performed the glorious trick of promotion once again, and this time nobody could snatch top-flight football away from them. Well, the other big teams could, of course, out on the field, and they duly did – but it was still glorious while it lasted.

STIRRINGS IN THE FOREST

Early in 1990 the Environment Secretary Michael Heseltine told the House of Commons that Thamesdown had been chosen as one of six areas in the country to be allowed to develop a community forest scheme. In fact the Great Western Community Forest is now

Lydiard Park is a staunch supporter of the community forest scheme. It seems that some of its residents are in need of a fresh injection of sap.

one of twelve areas of the country in which local people and organisations are working together to create a better environment, with plans to plant some fifteen million trees within the next twenty-five years; the first million have already taken root. The idea, quite simply, is to transform housing, business and shopping areas into places where trees will play an integral part in the environment; with so much new development on the outskirts of Swindon that is a massive task, but one that is already paying dividends. It also has the spin-off value of publicising why we need trees; no self-respecting school can ignore the project, while Forest Festivals in Old Town have brought the message right home to people's doorsteps. There is also the advantage, out on the fringes, of incoming companies being keen to be seen supporting both nature and the welfare of their workers and neighbours; Honda, for instance, 'keen to move towards a carbon balance', contributed £75,000 over three years between 1999 and 2001. Run by Swindon Borough Council, the scheme spills over into the conservation of ancient meadows, rivers, ponds and wetlands, and opportunities to get involved range from planting trees from seed to becoming a volunteer ranger. Michael Heseltine was an early supporter of the Millennium Dome, but is likely to be remembered with a great deal more approval for Britain's community forests.

THE BISHOP CENTENARY AWARD

In May 1992 the Victorian GWR Railway Village in the heart of town won the Bishop Centenary Award, which was set up to remind people of the good, the bad and the downright ugly in Swindon architecture. Built more than 150 years ago and restored by Thamesdown Council in the 1970s, it had been runner-up for the previous two years after the finalists had been voted for by the public. This time the village came ahead of two developments in West Swindon, the Intergraph and Renault buildings, and there was a sigh of relief in some quarters that the prize, not before time, had gone to a well-known project admired by tens of thousands of Swindonians, rather than to some splendid corporate development out on the fringes. 'It's good for the town,' said the Mayor of Thamesdown, Councillor Eric Smith.

A FAIR COP?

Wiltshire was among the first counties in Britain to use unmanned cameras to catch speeding motorists when legislation allowing their use came into force on 1 July 1992. Chief Inspector Roger Curtis said the cameras were expensive and would be used selectively: 'We will only put them on when everything else has failed. We hope that by advertising their presence we will be able to slow drivers down. These devices have been used in the United States and on the continent for years. It is only our innate sense of fair play that has prevented them from being introduced earlier.' The news had special meaning in Swindon where emotions were still raw after five young people had been killed senselessly in an accident in 1991 in Akers Way. Theresa Houghton, who founded the Moredon and Pinehurst Safety Group after the accident, welcomed the idea of cameras along that stretch of road. 'It would be brilliant, because there has been no change here,' she said. Ten years on, in the summer of 2002, the use of such cameras came under

The Railway Village: a worthy winner of architectural awards.

serious review, with calls to have them made far more apparent to motorists. Our 'innate sense of fair play' striking again?

It was a busy year for the police. Residents welcomed a police swoop at dawn on suspected drug dealers in Swindon, with thirty officers with sniffer dogs raiding five homes in Penhill. Three people were arrested and a quantity of 'substances' was taken away. A resident said drugs were sold regularly in half a dozen houses in the area: 'It's disgusting. The children around here are not safe. You find syringes by the road. You can't bring up kids in this atmosphere.' Superintendent Rodney Legg said: 'We have had a lot of information from residents who are tired of people dealing in that area. I hope that what we have done is a message to all those dealing in dangerous drugs in Swindon.'

RAISE A GLASS FOR TRADITION

The year 1993 brought the 150th anniversary of Arkell's, and the Swindon brewers did not let the chance for a year-long celebration pass them by. From the unveiling of a commemorative plaque to the launch of a new beer, an eye-catching mural to an open day, hardly a week went by without a nostalgic glance back to 1843. The company began the year as it meant to go on when former head brewer Don Kenchington raised a gold and black anniversary flag outside the brewery, to the accompaniment of a pair of Royal Yeomanry trumpeters. Looking on were three generations of Arkells, Peter, James and his fourteen-year-old eldest son George. The high spot, however, was the open day in September. It was the first in the company's history, and more than 1,500 people paid £2 a time to see what made a traditional brewery tick, and later to sample the finished product in the cellar bar. There was also an exhibition of photographs and breweryana, morris dancing and music, and a good old-fashioned Aunt Sally. Staff added to the atmosphere by dressing in Victorian garb, and chairman Peter Arkell, in his sideburns, succeeded in looking uncannily like portraits of his great-grandfather John. He even had founder John's tankard with him, a symbol of how much family ties and continuity meant to the firm. Everyone went home with an anniversary pint glass or mug, and you will still see them around people's houses in Swindon. With all the rush for change in recent years, the interest aroused by the Arkell's anniversary was a cheering reminder that there is still a place for tradition.

A BISHOP FOR SWINDON

Swindon failed to achieve city status in the twentieth century, and seems destined to wait a long time before it does so. Neither does it boast a cathedral, but a Church of England bishop it most certainly does have, in the form of the Right Revd Michael Doe. He became the first Bishop of Swindon in 1994, appointed as the suffragan or assistant bishop to the Bishop of Bristol, in whose diocese Swindon lies. The diocese is long and narrow,

The Bishop of Swindon, Michael Doe (second from left), blesses the expanded Rainbow Bookshop premises in 1998. (*Rainbow Bookshop*)

stretching along the M4 corridor between Bristol and Swindon. Traditionally, the suffragan was the Bishop of Malmesbury, but Bishop Barry Rogerson recognised the importance of a burgeoning Swindon by making the name change. In Michael Doe the diocese picked a radical thinker well in tune with Swindon and its problems. He chaired the town's well-argued but ultimately unsuccessful millennium campaign for city status, and is involved in a number of ecumenical and community initiatives. In the church nationally, he has responsibilities in the areas of church unity and world development, and is particularly interested in the church's response to the rich–poor divide and gender issues. After an academic training in theology and sociology, he began his ordained ministry in South London and then served as ecumenical youth secretary for the British and Irish churches. In the 1980s he was vicar of a local ecumenical partnership in Oxford, from where he went to be social responsibility adviser and a cathedral canon in Portsmouth. The bachelor bishop is also noted for his acerbic wit. When the humorist Miles Kington used 'the Bishop of Swindon' as a comic character in a newspaper column, clearly unaware that anyone with such an apparently outlandish title could possibly exist, the real bishop's riposte was every bit as entertaining as the original column.

FROM SMALL BEGINNINGS . . .

There were cries of 'cultural desert? What cultural desert?' as the first Swindon Festival of Literature was staged over a few days in May 1994. That said, it was not the most glittering line-up of all time. Michael Foot was there, plus the political whistle-blower Clive Ponting, Stanley Wells and the poets Ruth Fainlight, Sebastian Barker and Fiona Pitt-Kethley. A professor of Shakespearean studies at Birmingham University talked about the Bard, there was a residential writing weekend at Lower Shaw farm, and after that we were off to a jazz night at the Link Studio with the Clark Tracey Sextet. The annual kite festival at Lydiard Park was also on at the time. For the festival's ninth year in 2002, the speakers included Terry Pratchett, Mo Mowlam, John Humphrys, Will Self, David Lodge, Sarah Miles, Will Hutton, Linda Grant and Chris Woodhead. We would even have had Margaret Thatcher, had not her doctors famously gagged her just a few weeks before. There is no record of her having been present in 1994, shepherding Michael Foot around in his duffel coat.

In keeping with the town's cultural aspirations it was decided in the mid-1990s that the Brunel Centre was in need of a revamp – a task begun early in 1995 and completed more than two years later. The aim, apart from smartening the place up, was to pitch it towards the kind of town Swindon was seen to have become; the most obvious move up a social notch or two was the creation of a House of Fraser department store where the covered market used to be, with the market moved along to the striking-looking big top of a building close by – striking-looking but ultimately disappointing to newcomers from the North and Midlands, whose gut feeling that the South can't do markets properly has hardly been challenged here. This was by no means the end of work at the centre; a new Mall was introduced on the first floor in the Plaza, with plans for a connecting bridge between it and the Arcade. Mall, Plaza, Arcade, Centre: older shoppers have suddenly had to learn a new language. No longer can you get away with saying: 'Plaza? Which one's that again? They all look the same to me. Can't I just meet you on the corner where McIlroys used to be?'

Hospital Radio Swindon, broadcast in Princess Margaret Hospital and Princess Alexandra RAF Hospital in Wroughton, went back on the air in the summer of 1995 after six months' silence caused by the presenters' mixing desk blowing up. The desk was ten years old and had been unreliable for a year or so, but the final failure still came as a blow to the volunteers who manned the station. Most of the £6,000 needed for a new desk came through donations from local companies, and the brighter sound produced by the new system soon had the station's listener figures up again.

A series of spectacular sales in 1996 drew more widespread attention to the work of Dominic Winter Book Auctions, which first came to Swindon in 1988. Home Counties man Dominic abandoned his dreams of becoming an actor to learn the auctioneer's trade in Surrey and Bristol, and by the time he came to Swindon he was already specialising in books. His first premises occupied the ground floor of a terraced house in Victoria Road, with sales held at the Wiltshire Hotel. He then moved for two years to the Planks in Old Town, but for the past dozen years has been at Maxwell Street, in the old St Mark's Church of England School. Just an hour from London, he is regarded as a local by the book trade in the capital, and it is now accepted that when a rare book changes hands it is no surprise if it does so in Swindon rather than in New Bond Street. His record price is £190,000, or well over £200,000 with commission, for an album of collotypes taken by a group of Edinburgh gentlemen in 1848, the dawn of photography. He still feels obliged to Sotheby's and Christie's for turning down the opportunity to sell them before they came to him. Before that his record had been £32,000 for a book on the natural history of the Bahamas, with a series of very fine hand-coloured plates. 'I hate the thought of fine books being broken up for their plates, but I think people are coming to realise that a really good complete volume is now worth more than its parts,' he said. He is fascinated by the market for modern first editions, and not only because it often makes him money: 'It's so subject to fads and fashions, and you've got to be pretty sure of yourself if you put a lot of money into them. Some authors might be flavour of the month and have no staying power. Lots of people are putting money into detective fiction, but you've got to choose your authors very carefully.' Dominic has happy memories of selling the first James Bond book, *Casino Royale*, for £11,000, as he pursues what must be a very odd trade for this town. Or maybe not; with Book Club Associates and Readers' Digest now based in Swindon, there is a case to be made for its being the literary capital of Britain.

SHOPPING CENTRES

The shopping complex now known as the Great Western Designer Outlet was the UK's largest retail regeneration project when it was opened in March 1997 – a quite uplifting place with a hundred high street and other stores rubbing shoulders with gleaming pieces of industrial archaeology in splendidly restored Victorian buildings that once belonged to the GWR Works. Those who say 'it's all very well saving these buildings, but what do you actually *do* with them?' are shown the answer to that conundrum in no uncertain manner. The project was some ten years in the making and cost around £40 million to complete, and though few of us lie awake at night agonising over the fortunes of property developers let us hope that it is proving money well spent; that way we might see more of

Mementoes of the railways which once occupied its premises can be found everywhere at the Great Western Designer Outlet. Some people find the food hall alone worth the visit, with a real locomotive as its focal point.

this kind of thing up and down the country. The light and airy central food court, dominated by a genuine GWR locomotive in showroom condition, is as intriguing a place to eat as anywhere in Swindon or indeed miles beyond; and if you pick your moment there are times of day and days of the week when it is possible to move around the place almost blissfully free of crowds. Promoters of Swindon stress that the outlet centre is within 'easy walking distance' of town; if you are David Hempleman-Adams (another Swindonian) it is, but if you're pushing a buggy and pulling a toddler it seems rather further. At the end of the day, however, the town needs both main trading areas to thrive and prosper.

In January 1998 it was announced that McIlroys, the Regent Street store and Swindon institution, would close by June, and sure enough, on the last day of April it had gone, with the loss of 183 jobs. It had been founded in 1875 by Swindon man William McIlroy – Swindonians always said the name with the stress on the second syllable, the 'kill' – and for all but its first few years it occupied a prominent red-brick building whose clock tower was as much a landmark as the Town Hall, whose wrought-iron staircase was one of the high spots of Swindon architecture, and whose upstairs hall was a major meeting point for all but a century. This store was replaced by a more anonymous 1960s building, which in turn was demolished within weeks of closure to make way for the block now occupied by H&M fashions and other stores. There is still a clock, on the traditional corner, though it is obscured for much of the year by a plane tree. The closure of McIlroys was put down to competition from Debenhams, House of Fraser and the Great Western Designer Outlet Village, though a spokesman for the latter retorted that there

The McIlroys tower was so much a part of Regent Street that many older people viewed its demolition in the 1960s with disbelief.

The last rites at McIlroys, with
the smiles disguising what was
a very sad day for many. (*BUP*)

was no shortage of customers for all, 'but McIlroys has suffered from a lack of investment
and consistency of management in recent years'. The store was bought by Courtaulds
Textiles in the 1950s and put on the market again in 1995, leading to its acquisition by
the Scots-based fashion chain Mackays. Almost immediately, it seems, the move was seen
as a mistake, and a Mackays spokesman said: 'It has become increasingly apparent that
the operation of a single department store was not complementary to our core activity of
fashion retailing from smaller units.' On the last day staff wore blue T-shirts with the logo
'Gone But Not Forgotten', and many customers paid one last sentimental visit. 'A good,
old-fashioned store' was the verdict of one, and maybe that was ultimately McIlroys
downfall. On the other hand, there was a strange postscript to the story in June 1999,
when an independent survey of department stores placed it eighth in the national league
table of profitability in 1997.

SURVIVING MILLENNIUM NIGHT

The party of the decade? Of the century? Of all time? There was such a build-up to New
Year's Eve 1999 that the reality could never hope to live up to the expectation, in
Swindon or anywhere else. Neither did the millennium computer bug strike as had been
feared. For weeks before the big day the town's high-tech industries were boasting that
they were ready for any disasters that might threaten, but in the end even the most low-
tech, ill-prepared computer users sailed through the crisis unscathed. Staffing crises
seemed to pose greater problems for most, especially as there was a genuine influenza bug

around which seemed to offer the perfect excuse for those intent on sick leave on New Year's Eve, and administrators at Princess Margaret Hospital were especially anxious about what might lie ahead. In the event there were no high dramas there or anywhere else in Swindon.

Scare stories abounded about taxis being unprepared to turn out for under £150, waiters £100 and so on. Increasingly, as the day neared, drinks at home with a few friends or just the television seemed an increasingly sensible option. At the last minute the trendy Atrium restaurant in Havelock Square reduced its price from £85 to £20 in a bid to pull customers into a town centre that has no great tradition of letting its hair down on New Year's Eve. A few folk usually gather in Regent Circus to watch the town hall clock count down the minutes, but it is hardly carnival in Rio. As it turned out, Atrium and other central gathering places had a busy and jolly time of it, but all was fairly orderly, with just sixteen arrests made all over town. Plenty of people wore fancy dress, and a big contingent from RAF Lyneham made themselves heard at Yates's Wine Lodge. Somewhere a live band performed Gloria Gaynor's *I will survive* as the last seconds ticked away – perhaps not the most over-confident of sentiments with which to face the years ahead. All was far more calm at various churches throughout town, including Christ Church, where a ceremony of reflection was held and a two-foot square cake cut, to be shared over the weekend by Old Town residents. Christ Church grounds were also the scene of Swindon's millennium beacon, one of a thousand to be lit across the country. All in all it was a good night – but at the end of it, if Swindon was left thinking 'is that it, then?', it was by no means the only community to feel that way.

STEAM

The Steam museum, opened in June 2000 in former GWR Works property close to the Great Western Designer Outlet shops, has given Swindon the railway heritage centre it deserves. It is superb and beautifully done and as state-of-the-art as you would expect of anything that benefited from £8 million of Lottery heritage funding – but it also proves how hard it is to run a front-line exhibition centre in a provincial town. Swindon alone cannot keep a facility of this magnitude going; every man, woman and child in town would have to visit it twice a year, year after year, to do so. So the visitors from outside must be attracted in, and that opens up questions of tourism provision stretching far beyond the remit of a single attraction. You cannot fault Steam, and it is all here. Swindon was famous as a place where some of the best steam locomotives in the world were built, and the museum aims to give visitors the chance to experience the sounds, sights and smells of the Railway Works, and to hear the stories of the men and women who worked there. The tale of the Great Western Railway is also brought to life, from Brunel himself to some of the 70,000 staff the GWR employed at its height; a reconstructed station platform recalls the excitement of rail travel of old; and active workshops bring traditional skills to life. One of the aims of Steam was to help give Swindon a focal point, something about which it could be proud; it does all that, but in terms of keeping it going, Nobody Ever Said It Would Be Easy. On reflection, looking back over the century, that would be no bad motto for the whole town.

Acknowledgements

The text of this book was compiled with reference, thanks and all due acknowledgements to a wide range of sources. Pre-eminently, the files of the *Evening Advertiser*, chronicling the history of generations of Swindonians, have provided vital information and insights. *The North Wilts Herald* was the main reference point up to about 1930, and the regional *Western Daily Press* was also invaluable on stories of more widespread interest.

The following books were also read in compiling *Swindon in the News*, with all due acknowledgements: *English Journey*, by J.B. Priestley, Heinemann/Gollancz, 1934; *The Christ Church, Swindon Centenary Brochure, 1951*; *An Awkward Size for a Town: a study of Swindon at the 100,000 mark*, by Kenneth Hudson, David & Charles, 1967; *A Swindon Album*, Peter Sheldon, Red Brick, 1980; *Dors by Diana: an intimate self-portrait*, by Diana Dors, Macdonald Futura, 1981; *History of Bath Road Methodist Church, Swindon*, by E.R. Carter, 1981; *Gloucestershire Railways in the Twenties*, by Humphrey Household, Alan Sutton, 1984; *Bygone Swindon*, by Michael A. Howard, Phillimore, 1984; *Tramways Remembered: West and South West England*, by Leslie Oppitz, Countryside Books, 1990; *Swindon: History and Guide*, by John Chandler, Alan Sutton, 1992; *The Robins*, by Dick Mattick, Sporting & Leisure Press, 1993; *Arkell's Anniversary Album*, by Khadija Buckland, Red House, 1993; *The Silver Screen*, by Brian Little, Cinema Services, Bath, 1997; *Memories of Swindon*, True North Books, 1999; *50 Years of Swindon Speedway*, by Glynn Shailes and Robert Bamford, self-published, 1999; *A Century of Swindon*, Swindon Society, Sutton Publishing in association with W.H. Smith, 2000; *Steam: Museum of the Great Western Railways Guide*, English Life Publications, 2000; *The Old Lady on the Hill: the story of Christ Church, Parish Church of Swindon and its Community, 1851–2001*, by Brian Bridgeman and Teresa Squires, ELSP, 2001; *Nobody had Reverence: chapters in the life of Bill Bryant*, by Bill and Richard Bryant, self-published, publication date not apparent; *The Swindon Baptist Tabernacle*, by Sheila and David Pope, publication date not apparent; and various reports, brochures and leaflets published by Swindon Borough Council and its predecessors, and by individual visitor attractions and interest groups.

Photographs are largely by the authors or from their collection, but acknowledgements are also due to Chris Bowles, Tim King, Glynn Shailes, Steam, the *Western Daily Press* and the Alfred Williams Society.

Individuals and organisations to whom warm thanks are due are: Chris Bowles, Robert Buckland, the Richard Jefferies Society, Barry Leighton, Glynn Shailes, Jonathan Shorney and the Alfred Williams Society. The authors also thank the staff of the Tourist Information Centre in Regent Circus, Swindon, and most of all, the staff of the Reference Library at the Town Hall, Regent Circus.